W9-CME-557

THE CLEANSING OF THE HEART

THE CLEANSING OF THE HEART

VOLUME ONE

by

Barbara Dent

DIMENSION BOOKS
Denville, New Jersey 07834

First American Edition
by DIMENSION BOOKS INC.

First Published 1973
Copyright 1973 by Barbara Dent

For
the kingdom
and
for all those dear to me
who work for and in the kingdom,
especially ©

TABLE OF CONTENTS

Chapter

I shall pour clean waters over you and you will be cleansed; I shall cleanse you of all your defilement and all your idols. I shall give you a new heart, and put a new spirit in you; I shall remove the heart of stone from your bodies and give you a heart of flesh instead. I shall put my spirit in you, and make you keep my laws and sincerely respect my observances. You will live in the land which I gave your ancestors. You shall be my people and I will be your God. I shall rescue you from all your defilement.

—Ezekiel 36. 25-29

THE DEFILEMENT WITHIN

JESUS taught plainly that good and noble outward actions were the fruit of a well-ordered interior life centered on doing God's will. It was possible for a hypocrite to appear outwardly righteous while inwardly ruled by evil inclinations, but God had power to read the heart. No one could deceive him.

"Beware of false prophets who come to you disguised as sheep but underneath are ravenous wolves. You will be able to tell them by their fruits. Can people pick grapes from thorns, or figs from thistles? In the same way, a sound tree produces good fruit but a rotten tree bad fruit" (Matt. 7.15-18).

These hypocrites might make a great display of devotion and pious good will, but God cared only about their motives.

"It is not those who say to me, Lord, Lord, who will enter the kingdom of heaven, but the person who does the will of my Father in heaven" (Matt. 7.21).

The pure heart and surrendered will could alone produce a virtuous life.

"Brood of vipers, how can your speech be good when you are evil? For a man's words flow out of what fills his heart. A good man draws good things from his store of goodness; a bad man draws bad things from his store of badness. ... Anyone who does the will of my Father in heaven, he is my brother and sister and mother" (Matt. 12.34-35,50).

Always, he taught, we must look within, testing our motives, facing the truth, struggling to cleanse ourselves from self-interest, lawless desires and violent passions, for the outwardly conventional and respectable could be inwardly enemies of God and love.

"Can you not see that whatever goes into the mouth passes through the stomach and is discharged into the sewer? But the things that come out of the mouth come from the heart, and it is these that make a man unclean. For from the heart come evil intentions: murder, adultery, fornication, theft, perjury, slander. These are the things that make a man unclean. But to eat with unwashed hands does not make a man unclean" (Matt. 15.17-20).

Above all, Jesus condemned those who set themselves up as religious authorities, considering themselves the chosen of God, while in their hearts they were given up to the grossest forms of self-seeking and deceit.

As it was in Palestine in the time of Herod and Pilate, so it still is, and always has been all through human history. The fruits of the evil in men's hearts are inescapably there whatever records of the past we examine, wherever in the contemporary world we look for evidence. Mixed in with these fruits and

[6]

inseparable from them are all the evidences of the good that is also in men's hearts, struggling to express itself in countless ways.

The result is what can be a distressing ambivalence. Jesus himself warned it would be so, that the weeds and the useful plants would all have to be left growing together in one tangled mass until the final harvest time. Only then would God himself sort out and label rightly all the works and the hearts of mankind.

Because of this ambivalence, each of us on the personal level can lament with St. Paul, "I cannot understand my own behavior. I fail to carry out the things I want to do, and I find myself doing the very things I hate" (Rom. 7.15).

The interior war, what the ancients called the *bellum intestinum,* is there within all of us, and from it issue those wars between individual tribes and nations, and all those vicious impulses to maim and destroy, that mar the history of the human race. Were peace and love to reign in the hearts of each of us, they would also reign throughout the world. If each human being could respond to our Lord's words and be "blessed" because he is "pure in heart," (that is, with only one undeviating motive in life, to fulfill the two great commandments in obedience to God's will), then good would really overcome evil in every sphere of human activity.

[7]

But because man is what he is, a paradox, a split personality, a potential psychopath, history remains what it is

> Placed on this isthmus of a middle state,
> A Being darkly wise, and rudely great;
> With too much knowledge for the Sceptic side,
> With too much weakness for the Stoic's pride,
> He hangs between; in doubt to act, or rest;
> In doubt to deem himself a God, or Beast;
> In doubt his Mind or Body to prefer;
> Born but to die, and reasoning but to err;
> Alike in ignorance, his reason such,
> Whether he thinks too little, or too much;
> Chaos of Thought and Passion, all confused;
> Still by himself abused, or disabused;
> Created half to rise, and half to fall;
> Great lord of all things, yet a prey to all;
> Sole judge of Truth, in endless Error hurled!
> The glory, jest, and riddle of the world! [1]

Vatican II affirmed the same paradoxical element.

"The Church, embracing sinners in her bosom, is at the same time holy and always in need of being purified, and incessantly pursues the path of penance and renewal." [2]

"The truth is that the imbalances under which the modern world labors are linked with that more basic imbalance rooted in the heart of man. For in man himself many elements wrestle with one another. . . . He suffers from internal divisions, and from these

[8]

flow so many and such great discords in society. . . . Yet they (values) are often wrenched from their rightful function by the taint in man's heart, and hence stand in need of purification."[3]

The human condition, deriving from what Newman called "the aboriginal calamity," whatever or wherever that calamity was, remains one of perpetually marred efforts at betterment and continuous struggle to master an unruly self and environment.

It is as if there had been, incredibly far back in prehistoric times, a psychological and spiritual cataclysm in man, and from it derived a psychic fault line like those earthquake-prone weaknesses in the earth's crust. From this fault line in human nature come all the misuses of free will by which the races of mankind have disfigured their civilizations and cultures, spreading disharmony and hatred, instead of peace and love. Evil has proliferated so that each new generation is born, already catastrophe-prone, into a social environment that invites or manufactures disaster.

The outlook would be depressing were it not for the power of God's grace. It works within us, cooperating with our good impulses, and through us upon our world, to generate goodness and unselfishness and to oppose the forces of destruction with the creative Spirit of Love. This Spirit aims always at the establishment of the kingdom of heaven within the divided hearts that both long for and repel it.

St. Paul himself countered his lament over his divided self with faith's affirmation, expressed over and over again in his writings.

However the "fall" is interpreted, it can scarcely be denied by any realist that mankind is in a "fallen" or disoriented state. The disorderly and evil impulses within man war against his desires and efforts to do good and to love his fellows. Yet the Christian, no matter how clear-sighted and with what pain he acknowledges this human condition to be what it is, always hopes, always affirms God's power and intention to overcome evil with good.

Because he created man with free will, and has therefore made him capable of misusing his freedom, God, by means of his divine providence and his grace, works in devious ways. Mostly these ways are hidden from us, or are seen only partially and distortedly, but they are ever dynamically present.

We are exiles from the Eden of love — union with God, our true destiny. We are refugees from the kingdom of heaven within which alone we can find the peace and abiding love we seek. But we are not abandoned. Everyone who seeks, finds; and everyone who knocks, has the door opened. The inside of the cup, however defiled, can indeed be cleansed if we pray for and cooperate with God's grace.

To vary the fault line metaphor, we could say that at its origin the human race suffered a birth trauma. The shock of separation from innocence, from a state of union with God like that of a suckling with its mother, of being born into an equivocal freedom and knowledge, disoriented man. He became incapable of achieving, in his own powers alone, purity of heart, that is, undivided love, even while he compulsively craved it.

The history of the Jewish people and their continual unfaithfulness to God, their harlotry to idols, their promises and their betrayals of them, is a metaphor for the individual's inner instability. In it we see the drunken advance towards and recoil from God that exists within each one of us.

Because this is the human condition, all children born into it share it. The disease is handed on, generation after generation, through both heredity and environment. No parents can give their children perfect emotional security because no parents are capable of loving perfectly. No human institution can provide it either, because all are marred in some way or another since they derive from a marred source.

Psychologists may postulate that initially it is the birth trauma that makes the individual insecure emotionally, but this is only part of the truth. There would be no desire to return to the womb and its safety if parental love were perfect as God's love is perfect, and if the social environment, as the product of such a love, were permeated with harmony, justice, care for one another, and right values.

It is the human race itself that suffered the birth

[11]

trauma of severance from God, a God who through the ages continues to call to his lost ones, "Come back to me, my people!" It is only when separate members of that race come to their senses, as the prodigal son did, and acknowledge their plight for what it is, that hope becomes dynamic. The creative spiritual power, generated by the Holy Spirit in the hearts of those who consciously seek God and strive for that inward cleansing which alone can make them channels of his love for all mankind, is the one force that can change history.

All of our hearts are wounded and defiled. All need to be healed and cleansed, and only God can do it in the power of his grace. But first we must face our need and ask him to help us.

This sounds like a simple recipe, but it is in fact anything but easy to apply.

2

THE TWO SYNDROMES

IT is irrelevant whether we use traditional terms such as original sin, the loss of integrity, and concupiscence, or poetic ones such as the wounded heart, fatal flaw or dead men's bones. The fact remains that man is at war with himself and cannot be and do good with any ease. His interior defilement is a fact, and its source is sin.

The human race is enmeshed in what might be called the sin-suffering-evil syndrome. The extent and nature of the racial sin permeates the whole of humanity. We are all bound together both in sin and in salvation, for we are all in need of redemption and Christ became incarnate for us all.

God had a master plan for humanity, but sin scribbled all over it. God meant man to possess interior harmony and peace, to live in love and kindness with others, but sin brought suffering and the slow accumulation of evil to pollute the whole world. The sins of each man affect the race, the accumulation of the sins of the race affects each man. Thus a caricature is made of the world of right order and creative purpose that God intended.

Involved in the "death" of the first syndrome, we are rescued from it through the incarnation which makes us sons of God in the power and presence of the only-begotten Son. He gives us his "life," his grace, to replace the "death" we made for ourselves. Because of his gift we are able to become "righteous," which means to be cleansed of the inner defilement Jesus himself so accurately diagnosed and warned against.

This brings about "the real circumcision in the heart, something not of the letter but of the spirit" (Rom. 2.29).

Thus the Savior who rescues us from "the slavery of sin" in the first syndrome, makes it possible for us to enter into the "new life" of the second syndrome, that of love-suffering-prayer.

Suffering, so marked an element in the first syndrome, cannot be eliminated from this second syndrome for as long as we remain on this earth, for during that time our solidarity with the human race, enmeshed in the first syndrome, remains real. The second syndrome is our means of separating ourselves from the sin and evil of the first, insofar as these are present in our own inner beings, and of transmitting the suffering they cause into the redemptive suffering of Christ, in which he invites us all to share.

He proved his love for us by suffering to save us. The sufferings of his passion were the most powerful prayer for mankind of his whole life. His love, suffering and prayer were coalesced into that one redemptive act which brought us the life of God and the hope of glory.

[14]

But we must "share his sufferings if we are to share his glory" (Rom. 8.17). Through the second syndrome we become "dead to sin but alive for God in Christ Jesus" (Rom. 6.11). We enter a new kind of grace-imbued existence "so that as Christ was raised from the dead by the Father's glory, we too might live a new life" (Rom. 6.4).

This "new life" is already here in germ within our own hearts (in the process of being purified and made "righteous"), that everlasting life for which we, as immortal beings, are destined. Having turned away from the first syndrome, through our efforts to become ever more immersed in the second, we increasingly become one with Jesus, extensions of his incarnation, co-redeemers with him.

"Now, however, you have been set free from sin, you have been made slaves of God, and you get a reward leading to your sanctification and ending in eternal life. For the wage paid by sin is death; the present given by God is eternal life in Christ Jesus our Lord" (Rom. 6.22-23).

Now we can offer our "living bodies as a holy sacrifice, truly pleasing to God" (Rom. 12.2) because our whole existence is a participation in Christ, whose power at work in us is purging out the old corruption. This "sacrifice" is one with Christ's sacrifice for all mankind, for now we, "in union with Christ, form one body, and as parts of it we belong to each other" (Rom. 12.6).

[15]

Now "the life and death of each of us has its influence on others; if we live, we live for the Lord; and if we die, we die for the Lord, so that alive or dead we belong to the Lord" (Rom. 14.7-8). Our influence is no longer that of the first syndrome of hate and despair, but of the second one of love and hope.

That profound incapacity to love as we wanted to love, to do the good we yearned for and avoid doing the evil we hated, is now countered by the force of God's grace. As we learn more of the truth, which means learning humility, we become less pharisaical and hypocritical. The first syndrome engenders lies and deceit; the second truth and simplicity.

As we experientially discover, under the influence of the Spirit, what love means, we become more capable of putting love into practice. We become the "brothers and sisters and mothers" of Christ and of his extended mystical body, because we are doing the will of the Father through the second syndrome instead of our own perverted wills through the first. We increasingly become "good, honest men" in our hearts, instead of being "full of hypocrisy and lawlessness." Our fruits are those of the Spirit within us: "love, joy, peace, patience, kindness, goodness, trustfulness, gentleness and self-control" (Gal. 5.22). In the power of Christ we have at last been able to "crucify all self-indulgent passions and desires" (Gal. 5.24). We are learning how to conquer in the *bellum*

[16]

intestinum, and as a result are becoming forces for good in the social environment inself, since our hearts no longer willfully engender and pour forth "all manner of uncleanness."

There is now some hope that we can love both as emotionally secure and mature human beings, and also in a way that will foster such security and maturity in others. We can now perhaps achieve some success in fulfilling that basic human need to love and be loved.

Jesus assured us that he had come to give us more abundant life (John 10.10), and that this life would "turn into a spring inside us, welling up to eternal life" (John 4.14). We have only to "drink" of him in our thirst, and his Spirit will enter us to become "fountains of living water" (John 7.38). These will flow as the love of God itself from our hearts, indiscriminately, for all.

When this happens we shall be established in the second syndrome, and wherever we live bodily in the world, we shall take with us the kingdom of heaven itself in our hearts.

Our Lord spoke many parables about the kingdom of heaven; he also stated that it was within (Luke 17.21). In St. John's gospel, and particularly in the discourse at the last supper, it is recorded how he developed this theme of the interior life.

The theme had been announced in the very first chapter of St. John's book. Here we are told that

Jesus, the Word that was with God, the Word that was God, himself gives his own life to be men's light. This light of Christ, shining in the darkness of the first syndrome, is more powerful than it is. Become flesh and one with us, Jesus manifests to us his glory that is full of grace and truth, making known to us the Father himself (cf. John 1).

The purpose of this manifestation is to establish us in the second syndrome, love-suffering-prayer, which is the kingdom of heaven within. This is a spiritual reality whose fruits are expressed in time and space as we show forth tangibly and visibly, through loving kindness, the divine life God has placed in us. This is the flowing forth of the "fountains of living water" for a thirst-crazed world.

An examination of what Jesus says about love at the last supper shows the supreme emphasis he places on the need for us to love one another with his love, which is the love of the second syndrome.

Before eating, he washes the feet of his disciples. Then he says, "If I, then, the Lord and Master, have washed your feet, you should wash each other's feet. I have given you an example so that you may copy what I have done to you" (John 13.14-15).

This cleansing of the feet symbolizes the cleansing of the heart, the inner man, which can be a work only of Christ and his grace. But Jesus charges us to do it for each other. Thus he invites us to unite ourselves with the redemptive work of his passion, so that in his power we may be able to cleanse and help each other. The work of love that is his passion must be continued in time through us in our personal relationships.

As soon as Judas has gone out into the night to perform his work of darkness, Jesus says strangely, "Now has the Son of Man been glorified, and in him God has been glorified" (John 13.31).

Despite all appearances to the contrary, the passion is to God's glory, because it expresses the ultimate in self-giving love. Being redemptive, it has power to dissolve the first syndrome, and so it enables the kingdom of heaven to begin here on earth in the lovers of Jesus. It also opens the way into the eternal heaven of the resurrection, where the saints give glory to God because they are Christ's crown of victory.

Our Lord's words at the point where Judas is making the passion inevitable, affirm unquenchable hope. This hope he offers to those who enter into the kingdom of heaven within, so that they may overcome all their own hearts' darknesses and despair.

Jesus now says, "I give you a new commandment: love one another. Just as I have loved you, you also must love one another. By this love you have for one another, everyone will know that you are my disciples" (John 13.34-35).

Our love that is to be like his love has to include a share of that suffering for others that was his supreme act of love. This is what the second syndrome means.

The kingdom of heaven within, which is the kingdom of divine love itself, is thus extended into humanity to the glory of God.

The newness in Jesus' command lies in his stressing that our love is to be like his, that is, sacrificial. Our own hearts are to be immolated, as his was, disinterestedly and indiscriminately for the whole world. The more complete this immolation, the fuller the establishment of the kingdom of heaven within.

Such love is humanly impossible. As we try and fail, over and over, we learn this humbling lesson. The heart has to be cleansed, and only grace can do it. Faith comforts us with its assurance that with God all things are possible, even that we should be able to obey the command to love as Jesus loves. When we are finally humiliated into impotence, then God can and will work in us. Then he sends his Son to do our loving, suffering and praying in us, with us, for us.

Our passport into the kingdom of heaven within is Christ stamped on our souls, on our lives. St. John sees the blessed in heaven with the name of the Lord written on their foreheads. They are his, sealed with his seal, for eternity, but he began sealing them in time.

Jesus said, "Everyone who believes, has eternal life" (John 6.47). He used the present tense to signify that wherever Christ is, there is heaven.

At the last supper, he goes on to tell the disciples that he is going to leave them in order to prepare a place for them in his Father's house. He will return to take them there, by a way that they know. It is only in retrospect that they will understand his words.

Their way, like his, is to be the way of the buried grain of wheat that has to die in order to bring forth much fruit.

He says, "I am the Way, the Truth and the Life. No one can come to the Father except through me" (John 14.6). His way is the way of the cross, which is also the way of incredible love. The "truth" he is revealing is that loving, suffering and praying are the one act, the "way" to the Father. He himself is "the Truth and the Life" because he is the blueprint of what a man is meant to be, a man who is fulfilling the role for which he was made — loving — and so is fully alive.

He comes to us as "life" when we are "born anew" through the power of the Holy Spirit, as he explained to Nicodemus. Then he gives us what is his alone to give — eternal life and the kingdom of heaven within.

Earlier he had said, "I have come so that they may have life and have it to the full" (John 10.10). Now he says he *is* that life. This is the only life that is eternal, the only life we shall have in heaven. He offers us the chance of entering it within our own souls here and now.

"I am in the Father and the Father is in me. . . . It is the Father, living in me, who is doing this work" (John 14.10). Christ, our way to heaven, is also our revelation of the Father on earth and, in time, the proof of the Father's love. The Creator re-creates through the Son, and the Son invites us to share in this work of renewal. He reveals his complete oneness with God, and invites us to partake of it, to be the receptacles of "the Spirit of truth who will be with us and in us" (John 14.17).

Immersed in eternity while still in time, we shall know and "understand that I am in my Father and you in me and I in you" (John 14.20).

This is a clear promise of the indwelling of the Blessed Trinity in the human soul, of the establishment of what Jesus himself had called the kingdom of heaven within. It comes about because we love Christ, do what he wants us to do, and thus attract the Father's love, the Spirit's presence, and the Son's intimacy. We can never be alone or lonely, for God is with us.

"We shall come to him and make our home with him" (John 14.23). Anyone who makes our home his own lives with us in the closeness of the inner family circle, and where God is, there is heaven.

It is the Holy Spirit who will help us to understand and enter into these mysteries, and the peace they bring. "Peace I bequeath to you, my own peace I give you, a peace the world cannot give, this is my gift to you" (John 14.27). A heart that contains this peace must be a very different kind of heart from those "full of every kind of corruption" that our Lord inveighed against. It already tastes the peace of God that passes all understanding and that will pervade us in heaven.

Jesus goes on to explain that all our fruitfulness depends upon remaining one with him, as much one as the branches with the vine they grow from.

"Make your home in me, as I make mine in you" and so "bear fruit in plenty" (John 15.4,5), because "cut off from me you can do nothing."

This is a clear evocation of the human race incorporated into the incarnate Lord, so that by this union the second syndrome might render null the first. Only the Lord of history has power to nullify it, and we can overcome only with his power. The vine spreading out in its branches is the Savior on the cross opening his arms to embrace the whole world.

Risen, alive, active now in us, he will extend this embrace, using us for the enfoldment, to all, for it is the Father's will that all should be brought into the kingdom of love.

"Now the will of him who sent me is that I should lose nothing of all that he has given to me" (John 6.39) — this "all" is the human race.

The mysterious divine power pulsing through the hearts of those who remain in the love of the Lord, fructifies the whole world. It is the joy of heaven elevating the human into the exultation of the blessed and of the Trinity itself. It all comes about through love — not the crippled, divided love of the defiled

[23]

and the helpless human heart, the victim of the first syndrome, but the perfect love of God, active in such a heart once it is humbled and cleansed, and longing for the second.

The bearers of the fructifying life have been chosen and "commissioned" to "go out and to bear fruit that will last." This is the casting of the good seed over the whole earth, because we "love one another" (John 15.16,17). The love sown lasts on into eternity, is already eternity.

Opposed to this kingdom of heaven within, that is commanded to fructify the world, is the world itself, and all that expresses and clings to the first syndrome. "Therefore the world hates you" (John 15.19) — the horrifying, tangled ramifications of what pulses with evil, just as the holy vine pulses with love. Malice sets out to blight and kill the vine, and all who are the bearers of the kingdom of heaven within will surely suffer. Extensions in time and space of the eternal Savior, they will be persecuted as he was, but as part of the second syndrome that redeems.

In all this they will be strengthened, enlightened and upheld by the Advocate. They will be led "to the complete truth" (John 16.13), and he will speak to their hearts of the things of God so that they will not have to "ask any questions" (John 16.23); that is, he will infuse heavenly knowledge directly into their cleansed hearts.

Having been led by the Spirit into the kingdom of

heaven within, they have a special claim on God, for they are possessed by his own life.

"I tell you most solemnly, anything you ask for from the Father, he will grant in my name (John 16.23). This tremendous promise is for those who are fully alive with the vine's unique sap, and whose tendrils spread out only through the power of divine love, and in perfect faith that Jesus himself has "conquered the world" (John 16.33). Through the "trouble" spread by the first syndrome through all world events and all human hearts, is intertwined the vast, complex network of the vine. It binds all of humanity together, and counters the "trouble" with the secret, mysterious activities of divine providence, using human beings as its instruments.

In this vine, which is Christ and us joined to him, we are meant to find the peace he promises by entering deeper and deeper into his love. Peace comes when all conflict is stilled. All conflict is stilled when we are able to see human living as purposeful integration with Christ. Then everything we do and are becomes part of the kingdom of heaven within. It is given eternal purpose and creative power because it is part of his work as Savior, and he unites us with that work.

In his final prayer at the last supper, Jesus speaks to his Father in the intimacy of their love union. The stress is upon the transmission of the eternal life of the Father and Son to "all those you have entrusted to him" (John 17.2). The Father has given the Son "Power over all mankind" afflicted by the first syndrome, so that this life of heaven may be transmitted to them, leading them into the second syndrome.

Immersed in the divine circumincession, Jesus says, "I am not praying for the world, but for those you have given me, because they belong to you; all I have is years, and all you have is mine, and in them I am glorified" (John 16.9-10).

To glorify Jesus we must carry out successfully the work he gives us to do, yet we can do this only through the power he himself gives. In our ambivalent, fallen state, we remain impotent to glorify him; but united to the vine we can do all things. This means being united both to Jesus and to one another. Severance, discord, hatred, malice among ourselves is entirely incompatible with participation in the love union of Father and Son, with glorification of God.

"Holy Father, keep those you have given me true to your name, so that they may be one like us" (John 17.11), that is, united in the Spirit of Love. "I am not asking you to remove them from the world" — for we must remain in the human condition and affected by the first syndrome until we die, or else we cease to be human beings — "but to protect them from the evil one" (John 17.15) who manipulates a syndrome to separate us further and further from God and from the capacity to love.

To counter this, God sends the Son into "the world," and the Son sends us on the same mission of the salvation. We can carry out our mission only if "consecrated in the truth" (John 17.17) for only then will we be humble enough to want to be Christ's instruments. The first syndrome fosters lies and deceit. It encourages us to believe we do not need God, and can love and be happy to do good without him. Only the "truth" can show us our dependence upon Christ and our interdependence upon one another.

"Father, may they be one in us, as you are in me and I am in you, so that the world may believe it was you who sent me" (John 17.21). In this triple union the kingdom of heaven is established within the beloved of God, and its glory shines forth to irradiate the world, to compel belief, and to counter sin. The state of interpenetration is the fructifying state in which alone good works can be done.

The results are so dynamic that "the world will realize that it was you who sent me and that I have loved them as much as you loved me" (John 17.23). Now the "sound tree" manifestly brings forth "good fruit" (Matt. 7.18). Now the inside of the cup is gleaming clean, and reflecting the "light of the world" (John 9.5) for all to see.

This doctrine of the indwelling of Christ was developed by St. Paul and has been lived by all the Lord's "friends" ever since he rose from the dead.

[27]

What it promises is the only answer to our individual needs and those of the world. Its redeeming influence is the only one powerful enough to overcome evil and the first syndrome.

The heart in which the kingdom of heaven is established here and now, is the only heart which can have satisfied the innate craving to love and be loved, for it is able to love others with the selfless, exquisitely tender love of the Trinity, and it knows itself to be loved likewise by that same Trinity.

3

THE DARK NIGHT OF THE
HEART AND WILL

OUR Lord sets before us the ideal of perfect love and the duty to strive for it. He summons us to the kingdom of heaven within, and union with the Blessed Trinity. We long to respond to his call, yet when we try, we find ourselves most pitifully inadequate and helpless.

In those hearts where the kingdom of heaven is fully established, there can be no darkness and no evil, but it takes many, many years before the risen Christ's conquest of the darkness and evil within us is complete.

Why does it take so long? What are the chief obstacles we place in his way? How best can we cooperate with grace? Exactly what is it that he wants us to renounce for his sake?

First it must be made plain that purification of the heart and purification of the will are inseparable. We equate the heart with those affective powers that all normal people have. They are the psychological and emotional equipment with which we relate to other people. They can be of tremendous use to us in our loving, but they can also be a hindrance for, because of the fall, they are not under the control of the will, and so are often expressed in wrong ways and for wrong reasons.

They incorporate desires and passions of great intensity that can become directed towards what is opposed to the establishment of the kingdom of heaven within. They can also raise such a storm in us that we are deaf to the enlightenment the Spirit is trying to give us. They can enslave us in obsessions and compulsions associated with them, so that we are severed from the peace of God and lose all desire for spirituality.

If right order prevailed, these affective powers would all be under the control of the will, responding to what it indicated were the right things to love, and loving them in the right way with the right emphasis. In other words, our hearts and wills would then be operating in accordance with God's will and its purpose of harmonious, unifying love for the universe.

Love is proved not by any emotions we may or may not have, but by the union of our wills with God's will and our readiness to sacrifice ourselves for others. Jesus exhorted us to keep the commandments and do the Father's will in all things, as he himself did. It is irrelevant whether we derive pleasure from this or not.

Primarily, love is not a feeling, a function of the affective powers, but a choice, an operation of the will. We must choose to love, no matter how we feel about it, and prove the sincerity of our choice in sacrificial action. Wherever scripture speaks of unclean hearts, it means wills that have strayed from God's will, allowing the affective powers to become idolatrously involved with creatures, instead of directing themselves first to the Creator, and subsequently to creatures for his sake.

Unless insane or feeble-minded, we have always some freedom of choice, and are bound to use it to coincide with God's will for us. Though to some degree victims of our own buried lives and involuntary desires, we can still exercise whatever freedom we do have to choose God's will as we see it, and invite the action of his grace, with a consequent enlargement of our area of freedom as grace penetrates and controls both will and heart.

We carry about with us a great burden of encumbrances and attachments — we must shed them all for love of God.

When Jesus promised at the last supper that he would be in us, and we in him, he meant we had to make room for him. This means the labor of casting out all the rubbish we cling to and cherish. He can enter only as far as we invite him, having emptied ourselves to receive him.

The dark night of the heart and will is this emptying-out of self and flowing-in of Christ.

We enter this dark night only when we truly and fully dedicate ourselves to God, turning with determination from all sin, serious and trivial. We must even resolve to eliminate, with God's help, whatever imperfections grace reveals to us. This is the initial movement by which the heart and will choose God and right order, the choice being made because all that belongs to the first syndrome has been understood and hated as anti-God.

As a result of determining to put God first, we encounter a bitter conflict with our own selfish desires, drives, needs, longings for self-satisfaction and emotional cravings for fulfillment other than the spiritual. The ensuing battle reveals to us our humiliating helplessness, our nothingness and our need of grace.

We begin to go without, persistently and ruthlessly, for the sake of the kingdom of heaven within.

As we go deeper into the night, we are gradually separated from wrong desires, or from desiring wrongly, by the combination of our own efforts to jettison rubbish, and God's direct action by grace in what are aptly called the "passive purgations."

For a long time we may seem to drift, feeling anchorless and empty, while the will is renouncing pleasures and possessions formerly hankered after for their own sakes, but which now seem hollow and trivial. Because the heart is longing for God and his kingdom within, but is not yet pure enough to receive what God offers, it endures a most painful state of dispossession and despoliation, usually for many years. During this time of purification, we may serve and love God in an aridity so complete that it seems to mock that service and love. We may even endure a black midnight of desolation and abandonment when it seems the very God we yearn for intolerably, himself spurns and mocks us.

It is sadly true that if the fallen human heart were to derive emotional satisfaction and sensible joy out of its loving and serving, it would always seek these lesser goods for their own sake, rather than God himself for no other reason than that he is God and summons us. Not until it has been purified and right order has been reestablished, can God safely give it such graces.

Only through complete purity of intention can we reach the kingdom of heaven within and the "freedom of the sons of God." The defiled human heart and the divided human will tend always to appropriate things and say "mine" over them. Cluttered with the "treasure" it has accumulated and gloats over, the fallen heart cannot reach God without a complete re-education.

The truth that "makes us free" (John 8.32) is that we do not, cannot, own anything, including ourselves. God owns all, and entrusts the usage of things to us. To use them rightly, we must always aim not at our own self-satisfaction but at the honor and glory of God. What cannot be used or owned for God's honor and glory must be renounced in the dark night of the heart and will, if we are to enter into the fullness of the kingdom of heaven within.

"It is necessary that every appetite and taste be renounced, if it be not purely for the honor and glory of God, and that you remain in emptiness for the love of him who in this life did not desire to do more than the will of his Father, which he called his meat and drink."[1]

The heart is imperfect and to some degree defiled until this state of complete despoliation is attained. It must acknowledge its debased state and open itself to God's action because to be made clean is to the honor and glory of God.

There is to be no bargaining, no sales-talk, no account-making, but one simple, continual act of loving self-abandonment. God is invited in — then we let him act, while we, merciless to all manifestations of self-will and self-love, cooperate with his action.

The cleansing of all base desires has to extend even into "the pains and afflictions of the secret places of the desires,"[2] that is, into the depths of the subconscious where we keep repressed some at least of what influences our conscious behavior and urges.

The fault line from the fall runs right through these hidden depths, and their volcanic forces are too often expressed irrationally and destructively, causing suffering and preventing single-minded assent to God's will. All hidden desires of a base or uncontrollable nature that have become implanted in us, their roots concealed by our imperfect heredity and environment, have also to be given up by being made subject to God's grace. It is he alone who can harness their force to his own honor and glory, directing them in accordance with his will.

We must submit to and cooperate with this action of God in faith, and that faith itself is purified in the process, for it is beyond the understanding of the intellect and rational mind.

"Naked I came from God, and naked will return." We begin to understand what Job meant. All we can take to God when we go on that last journey, is our love of him, and even this has come about only through his grace. We glimpse what the spirit of poverty really is – it is not to need or want created things, but only the Creator. It is not to need or want any means by which to go to God, but only God himself, naked spirit to Spirit.

"For that reason we call this detachment night to the soul, for we are not treating here of the lack of things, since this implies no detachment on the part of the soul if it has a desire for them, but we are treating of the detachment from them of the taste and desire, for it is this that leaves the soul free and void of them, although it may have them; for it is not the things of this world that either occupy the soul or cause it harm, since they enter it not, but rather the will and desire for them, for it is these that dwell within it."[3]

In order to be born again in the risen Christ, the human heart, because of its defilement, has to go down with him into the dark tomb of nothingness and dispossession, where it dies finally to self. Just as the pattern of the incarnation is parabolic – God descending in Christ into matter, dying in his human form, rising and ascending again, so our own progress in love is parabolic. Our hearts have to descend from the worldly happiness of pleasures and possessions they naturally cling to, into a dark night of discipline and slow renewal where there is suffering, groping and loss.

From this they slowly rise again into the glory of Christ, as his presence in them becomes more and more pronounced. He fills the void created by the mortification of self-love and self-will, and "makes his home" in the place that has been cleansed for him. Finally, at the summit of love, the heart, filled with the Holy Spirit and temple of divine love, is transformed. "And we, with our unveiled faces reflecting like mirrors the brightness of the Lord, all grow brighter and brighter as we are turned into the image that we reflect; this is the work of the Lord who is Spirit" (2 Cor. 3.18).

This process of denudation and renewal is purgatorial. In fact, it is purgatory. It usually lasts a lifetime and in most cases will be concluded only after death, for the human heart and will are rebelious and very difficult to reduce to submission.

Most of us like the idea of sanctity, but do not really want to pay the full price for it. We are like St. Augustine praying for purity, but not just yet. Total love appeals to us, but not if we have to give up anything much in exchange for it.

Consequently, many enter the dark night of the heart and will partially or temporarily, but few persevere to the end when "all self-indulgent passions and desires" (Gal. 5.22) are purged out, and they can say with St. Paul, "I live, now not I, but Christ lives in me."

It is to attain this condition of total love and union with Christ in simplicity, as opposed to the fallen human condition of fragmented love, divided purpose and misdirected desire, that we enter upon the dark night of the heart and will. We shall endure it to the end only in the strength of God's grace and the growing power of Christ within.

4

RENUNCIATION AND MEDIOCRITY

JESUS said,
"If any man comes to me without hating his father,
mother, wife, children, brothers, sisters, yes and his
own life too, he cannot be my disciple" (Luke
14.26).

This apparently immoral statement, seeming to
contradict the commandment to love, is really a
reiteration that the "first and great commandment"
to love God is emphatically the first one. God has to
take precedence. We love others for his sake, and we
love them perfectly only with the love that he gives
us.

Most natural attachments of the heart such as
those listed above by Jesus, are a mixture of good and
bad, of self-seeking and genuine giving. They are not
entered into only for the honor and glory of God, but
for a number of mixed motives arising from our
ambivalent inner condition.

In order to arrive at loving only for the honor and
glory of God we have to "hate," that is, detach
ourselves from all the satisfactions and desires connected with these natural relationships. Although
they are a necessary part of human living and of the
human race's continuation, and are therefore good in
themselves, concupiscence prevents us from keeping

them in proportion unless God helps us. We must somehow disengage ourselves from them in order to be the Lord's disciple.

This does not mean being cold and indifferent, but being detached, which is the necessary condition for loving disinterestedly. The same kind of truth is contained in our Lord's paradox, "In order to save his life, a man must lose it."

We must not be enamored of anyone or anything except God. We must renounce that bitter-sweet fascination of being in love. We have to resist its power to draw and enthrall our desires. We must not give people or things the right to enslave us. We have to say "no" to *la belle dame sans merci,* for her charms are fatal.

I saw pale kings and princes too,
    Pale warriors, death — pale were they all!
They cried — "La belle Dame sans Merci
    Hath thee in thrall!"

I saw their starved lips in the gloam
    With horrid warning gapéd wide,
And I awoke and found me here
    On the cold hill's side.

With a poet's intuitive insight into the truths of the human psyche, Keats saw that to be snared by created beauty, by the romantic ideal, was to permit one's spiritual lifeblood to be sucked away.

Normally the romantic sees something noble and

desirable in being thus captive, but in the above poem Keats depicts the tragedy of the situation. The tragedy is not confined to romantic love between the sexes, for such romanticism exists in any human relationship where there is idealization, obsessive fascination, and desire to immolate oneself in some manner to a human idol.

The dark night of the heart consists in the mortification of desire in *all* things, St. John of the Cross teaches. He speaks of the heart's unfaithfulness or divided purpose by saying that it "stays and pastures on other strange pleasures" wanting "to intermingle desire and affection for other things" rather than to be "content with God alone" and with his love.[1]

It is only in the night of full renunciation that the heart can attain singleness of purpose and eliminate self-seeking. In thus making of itself an altar, on which self-love is immolated, it is loving as Christ does, that is, in a sacrificial manner. It has given up all idol-worship to make God its only object of adoration.

Because its love is sacrificial it has only one desire, to see and do God's will at whatever cost to itself.

The demand for complete renunciation and total love seems so cruel that few Christians respond fully to it. In a competitive, materialistic society, run by the profit motive, the odds are high against spirituality. If it is hard to be detached about material things, it is even harder to renounce the heart's attachments to people, and yet to go on loving through the grace of God.

So complex is the psychology of our human relationships that it is possible to be blind to a love that is fastening us to mediocrity, and even to believe that it is our greatest virtue. Only the remembrance that our hearts are innately depraved, and have an involuntary impulse to give in to mediocrity, to seek satisfaction in the created instead of in the Creator, to eat the forbidden apple under the delusion that it will elevate us to beatific heights, will give us enough caution to be suspicious of "the holiness of the heart's affections" (Keats again).

Christianity has never pretended that to conform perfectly with Christ's command to love as he loved is easy, yet it has not compromised with the ideal. In fact, our Lord himself warned that anyone who compromised was not worthy of the kingdom of heaven. The foolish virgins were shut out. So was the guest without a wedding garment. The man so busy filling his barns died that very night under unfortunate circumstances. There was no time for a disciple to go back and bury his dead. The unforgiving servant was "handed over to the torturers till he should pay all his debt." The house built on sand collapsed in ruins.

It is human nature to hear God's call to total love and renunciation, for after all that is why he gave us ears; it is also human nature to become so busy counting the possible cost that we answer with only a half-hearted murmur, "I may come — probably tomorrow," or perhaps refuse, "I'm busy now for an indefinite period. Call again later."

Even those who respond generously and enthusiastically — "As Jesus was walking on from there he saw a man named Matthew sitting by the customs house, and he said to him, follow me. And he got up and followed him" (Matt. 9.9) — seldom improve on that initial enthusiasm, or even manage to maintain it. In the first fervor of dedication, they are sincerely convinced that they want to make the total response, say the uncompromising "yes," yet they often fail to continue through the years without surrounding that initial gift with reservations and elaborate systems of self-protection. They want to give, but their flawed human nature, their fallen hearts, played upon by the devil, and vitiated by their own weaknesses, force them into mediocrity.

Divided purpose in us seeks to evade the consequences of total commitment, and in the process often develops compromise into a fine art. However fashions change, whatever way out forms theological speculations adopt, the call of Christ to each individual remains the same, and its demand total. A true response to this call, whatever mode of life it involves, must lead to affirming with St. Paul, "For me, to live is Christ."

[42]

Whatever the vocation, celibate or married, there can be no essential self-fulfillment apart from Christ. We discover our true selves as we become those particular extensions of his incarnation that he has chosen us to be. Any apparent fulfillment that occurs in alienation from Christ is spurious and dependent upon factors that chance can shatter, and usually does.

Any route to God is straight and narrow with Calvary an inseparable part of it. The married state is no easier than the celibate *if* it is entered into as one's peculiar and God-indicated route to him. Of course this is often not the case, whereas the celibate's choice is usually a deliberate and conscious dedication to Christ first and foremost.

The total love that God demands is incarnated in Christ himself, and only in Christ. It can express itself through human lives when infused into them as an extension of the divine life itself, those living waters, that indwelling of the Trinity, that our Lord promised to those who love him. It means a passionate, uncompromising involvement of the whole self with the whole self of the personal, living, triumphant yet gloriously wounded risen Lord.

The human heart, disintegrated and flawed as it is, naturally fears such complete involvement with both God and man.

We want to preserve intact the ego with all its intravenous systems for feeding self-satisfaction and

[43]

self-preservation. We cannot help fearing and repelling such an invasion of the Other, although without it the enchained ego cannot be released into the freedom of the sons of God.

We are prisoners who have become dependent upon the enclosure of our cell walls for our sense of security. Just as the trumpet blast shattered the walls of Jericho, so would the blowing of the Holy Spirit upon our pitiful ramparts raze them finally — if we let it. "For he bursts the gates of bronze and shatters the iron bars" (Ps. 106.16).

We recoil from even the thought of encouraging such invasion. The ego is certain it would mean disaster. Its instinct for preservation rebels against the dissolution of its barriers.

Such fears are involuntary. They are part of the complex defense mechanism against God that is born with us. We cannot help our myopic way of looking at things, our instinctive reaching out for half-truths, our intense anxiety at being taken over by God, our dread of him as an alien, destructive force instead of our loving, eternal Father.

What is required of us is the calm recognition of all such systems of evasion, and the willed construction in the power of divine grace of contrary systems of encouragement. We are called upon by God to recognize the insidious nature of the temptation to mediocrity, of the urge to compromise. We have to counter it by persistent prayer for his help, by the will to give and receive all, and by actions which express that will.

"I believe nothing can happen that will outweigh the supreme advantage of knowing Christ Jesus my Lord. For him I have accepted the loss of everything, and I look on everything as so much rubbish if only I can have Christ and be given a place in him. . . . All I want is to know Christ and the power of his resurrection and to share his sufferings by reproducing the pattern of his death" (Phil. 3.8,10).

This must be what we consciously will in opposition to our involuntary desires and schemings to retain our walls, to refuse "the loss of everything."

The temptation to mediocrity is essentially a temptation to choose comfort by evading tension, stress and battles in favor of security and safety. This can lead to petrification, through repression and circumvention, of a person's whole affective powers. The personality becomes sterile, dehydrated, protected by a complex system of evasions and compromises, the real person who was meant to be reborn into Christ through total dedication and "undivided attention to the Lord" (I Cor. 7.35) gone to earth from sheer lack of encouragement.

Alternatively, the affective powers, instead of being stifled, may be diverted. Then our life and passion become centered on substitutes: liturgical niceties, research, career, art, some hobby, administration, power, antiques, aesthetics, business, sport, relatives, or one other particular person. They may even become fixated on some such mundane and irreligious activity as golf, racing or dog-breeding.

The temptations to compromise over the demands of total love and complete renunciation are many and dangerous. The celibate is perhaps more open to them than the person whose vocation is marriage. In marriage, if it is a dedicated Christian one, total love is also demanded by God, but its channel is the marriage partner and the children of the union, there in the flesh, obvious, defined and inescapable. For the celibate the channel, being the human family loved and served in, for and by means of Christ, is much more easily mistaken or wrongly labeled or simply ignored just because it is so ubiquitous.

The human family means not some nebulous abstract, but real persons whose abrasive presence and perpetual demands cannot, and are not meant to be, evaded. In all cases it is people, individuals, persons, actual living, palpitating entities who cannot be avoided, and with whom contact must be made in some fructifying way if Christ is to be served and honored, if divine love is to be fulfilled.

The whole of humanity is one organism, and this organism is the Body of Christ in the process of being incarnated. Through it we are meant to confer the sacrament of love upon one another. Through it we can, on the contrary, by hate and sin shut off

ourselves and others from participating in this sacrament of love.

The temptation to mediocrity suggests that the
living waters in our hearts should be turned into a
stagnant lake of self-enclosure by blocking off the
channels by which God's love pours into it and the
outlets that are meant to pour it out again upon
others. In time the whole place becomes "a fen of
stagnant waters,"[2] with the affective powers choked.

"They have abandoned me, the fountain of living
waters, only to dig cisterns for themselves, leaky
cisterns, that hold no water" (Jer. 2.13). To dig a
cistern for oneself means to construct it with the
intention of not sharing it with others.

Also evident where mediocrity threatens is the
"one for you, and one for me" trading mentality. The
person considers that in return for his gift of himself
to God, God owes him certain satisfactions, comforts,
consolations, successes, recognitions, rewards. If he
does not get what he believes is his due he becomes
sour, bitter, self-pitying, cynical, savagely critical
(perhaps of the Church as "a juridical institution.)).
He is a disappointed man who feels he has not been
valued and recognized at his true worth, and someone
or something must be made to suffer for it.

He has forgotten that the initial total gift of self
made to God when he began to enter the dark night
of the heart and will, was a form of interchange by

which he accepted in return, and unquestioningly, whatever God chose to give him.

Total love means embracing what God gives and lets happen, that is, his will, as the token of his loving kindness and the means of both one's salvation and sanctification, and also one's redemptive work for others. We accept, welcome, absorb, in faith and loving trust. There can be heroism here, unavoidable majesty of selflessness that can register on the ego as its contrary — humiliation, defeat, squirming self-seeking. God's gifts and their effects are often paradoxical, and recognized as good only by means of faith.

The "one for you, one for me" temptation is aimed at making one repudiate or avoid suffering and the dark night of the heart, that death of self, that burying of the seed, from which alone can emerge the risen self in the power of Christ's own resurrection, and hence the crowning of total love.

It is well to remember that "God's gift was not a spirit of timidity, but the Spirit of power, and love, and self-control" (2 Tim. 1.7).

There is also the temptation to succumb to mediocrity in personal relationships, avoiding intimacy and the pain of self-revelation and of receiving the confessions and love of others. In such relationships honesty is avoided in favor of polite half-truths, soothing evasions, and surface agreements, these being rationalized as kindness or even Christian charity. Those blinding moments of truth in which we acknowledge how we use others (and they us), how we are run by our mechanisms of self-interest by which we feed secretly on those we profess to love most sincerely, are repudiated. Instead are chosen the sly prevarications that assure us we are good mixers and not the type to give offense to anyone, and that this is the best way to be.

Mediocrity can also be succumbed to in our relationship with ourselves. We have to love ourselves as God loves us, but this does not mean self-indulgently excusing ourselves. Rather it involves a pitiless self-honesty in which we pray fervently for the grace to face ourselves as we are.

There can be no mediocrity regarding self-knowledge. If the truth that God offers, together with the grace to bear it, is accepted when and how he offers it, interior humiliation is inevitable. Christ sets out to invade and permeate the life and the heart dedicated to him, and this means progressive insight into the unchristed self down to its demon-haunted depths, which have to be cleansed by the passive purgations.

It means the painful relinquishment of all masks, all comforting illusions, all evasions of reality, all dramas, all role-playing. Christ is truth. He is also light. Where he is, lies and darkness cannot also be, yet the unredeemed personality and defiled heart are steeped in these. Total love becomes a reality when the heart has refused the temptation to mediocrity in one's relationship with oneself, to choose instead

Christ's invasion and powers of transformation no matter what that involves.

The mediocrity temptation also presents itself as one to self-cosseting. Having renounced so many desires and pleasures for love of God, we may decide we have a right to pamper ourselves a little here and there by way of compensation. There are legitimate pleasures, necessary relaxations, prudent concessions to our own acknowledged weaknesses. The danger is when these are indulged as a result of self-pity or a desire to make up to ourselves for renunciations once made but now secretly regretted or envied in others. In other words, when we seek substitute satisfactions for what is denied to us because of the Christian vocation to sacrificial love, we are compromising with that vocation.

A traditional name for mediocrity is acedia, or spiritual sloth. There is an old-fashioned ring about such terms which inclines some to dismiss them and what they stand for as irrelevant to modern life and post-Vatican II spirituality. Yet Vatican II documents themselves affirm the ancient call to total love, and hence to a war against all forms of mediocrity.

Our Lord never demands less than everything. The temptation to mediocrity invites compromise, but the heart that truly seeks Christ goes down willingly into its dark night, and lets itself be stripped of everything but God.

MARTYRDOM OF THE HEART

IF, in the dark night of renunciation, we consecrate our hearts to Christ, so as to enter fully into his passion with him as it takes place in the vine, what form is our interior martyrdom likely to take?

Martyrdom means witnessing to Christ in love to the point of being killed for one's faithfulness. The first recorded martyr, Stephen, died as his Lord did, praying for those stoning him to death, those who had "put down their clothes at the feet of a young man named Saul."

The grace that led to Saul's conversion into the apostle Paul came to him through the man he helped martyr. "The blood of martyrs is the seed of Christians" because the giving of one's life as a witness to Christ is an act of such perfect love that it impels the divine sap of grace to course abundantly through the vine. This brings about the spiritual renewal of many and the triumph in unitive love of others.

But martyrdom does not have to be an outward and obvious shedding of blood resulting in death. It can be inward and secret, a slow process going on over many years, culminating in a faith and love as powerful and vitalizing as that of the slain martyr.

[51]

Our Lady was a martyr, but she did not die for her Son in any visible way.

For us, interior martyrdom is the practice of detachment from all that could deflect us from total love, and the entering into an attachment to Christ so complete that he captures our whole being. Its motive is love of both God and neighbor, and a desire to be wholly identified with the Lord as Savior. It is the reversal into right order of the disorder in our fallen natures. Its whole purpose is to purify our hearts until we cry, "I love – now, not I, but Christ loves in me!"

There was, of course, never any disorder in Christ's being, never any need to learn detachment or achieve the right kind of attachment. His was a perfectly harmonious nature permeated by perfect love perfectly expressed. Yet he, being our way to the Father, and like us in all things except sin, went through the process of the grain of wheat falling into the ground and dying, in his perfect human nature, so as to make it possible for us to do the same in our imperfect human nature and our defiled human hearts.

Our affections play a very prominent part in our lives, but because our nature is wounded, they are mutinous, attaching themselves inordinately and wrongfully, seeking emotional and carnal satisfaction for its own sake, and pulling us away from God instead of towards him. What should be free of self-interest is contaminated by it in all kinds of ways that only the light of grace can fully reveal to us. This goes for both our affective relationships with other people and with God. We are the victims of "the tyranny of corruption" so that we "groan in our hearts" as we wait to enter into "the glorious freedom of God's sons" (Rom. 8.21-23), in which all our loving will be part of "the love of God which has been poured out in our hearts by the Holy Spirit whom we have received" (Rom. 5.6).

Through martyrdom of the heart the affections, all in dark disorder in our fallen nature, are restored to enlightened right order, and the whole love of the heart is directed to its one true end, God, through the doing of his will. We learn to love the right people and things in the right way, for God's sake, and the heart rejoices "only in that which is purely the honor and glory of God."

"For the whole business of attaining to union with God consists in purging the will from its affections and desires; so that thus it may no longer be a base, human will, but may become a divine will, being made one with the will of God."[1]

After the death of self-love we enter the risen life of Christ, and become the temples of God, "heirs of God, sharing the inheritance of Christ, only we must share his sufferings, if we are to share his glory" (Rom. 8.17). Now we can say, "The love of God has been poured out in our hearts by the Holy Spirit, whom we have received" (Rom. 5.5). Thus the martyred heart becomes the glorified heart, and the long torture of detachment ends in attachment to nothing but Perfect Love himself. The human heart, through the abundance of living water poured into it from the Sacred Heart, becomes the unobstructed channel for the spreading of Christ's love into the world.

Of all human beings, Mary is the heart's supreme model. Born sinless, always full of grace, in every way controlled by the Holy Spirit, there was never any disorder in her loving, so there was no need for her heart to be martyred in order to restore right order to her affections. From the first she brought forth God's love, and only his love, into the world – visibly in the embodied Christ formed from her body, and spiritually in the perfection of her identification with her son. So complete was this, that she went through an interior crucifixion equivalent to his bodily one. In a unique way, she became a co-redeemer with him, "fitted into the pattern of his death," making up with her own sufferings "what is lacking in the sufferings of Christ, for the sake of his body, the Church" (Col. 1.24).

The complete redemptive act is Christ's plus that of the vine of Christ-humanity, and in her part in this act Mary, among humans, excelled all other humans because of the perfection of her love.

So the human heart, in the process of its martyrdom, has as its model Mary's heart, and as its refuge, source of grace, and ultimate meaning, the Sacred Heart. Its way has to be through the passion of Jesus where, by meditation, prayer, love and acts of the will, it merges its own sufferings purposefully with his.

According to the plans of the divine providence and the generosity of the sufferer, the martyrdom is longer or shorter in time, and of greater or lesser intensity. What is certain is that it cannot be evaded by anyone dedicated to Christ, and that God is likely to use whatever material is at hand in this purification, that is, those closest in blood ties, friendship, and love relationships of various kinds, together with the temptations and attractions arising from life around us. Wherever the heart is attached, limpet-like, to a beloved, there God's abrasive action will be felt, until love becomes so selfless that it can give itself "purely for the honor and glory of God". Family relationships are not exempt from this rule, as is shown by what St. Thérèse went through in the process of supernaturalizing them.

However, there are not many among those immersed in ordinary marriage and family life, and the concerns of the temporal order, who will ever seek or submit to martyrdom of the heart. It will come to them, as a rule, only if God has made himself very real to them in some way, and called them in a clear and recognizable manner; or if they have really faced the problem of human suffering, and sought in dumb and helpless agony to find in Christ a meaning for it all. Such people are thus sensitized by God to eternal values, and they are not as likely to recoil from the passion and all its implications as do those who are happily immersed in the normal satisfactions and spiritually anaesthetizing pleasures of life.

Usually, those who experience interior crucifixion will be those who live in consecrated celibacy, with the aim of giving themselves wholly and directly to Christ. But even among these, the temptation to compromise is persistent, and a grace of special generosity is needed for total oblation.

Yet it is obvious that both Jesus and Paul are speaking to all Christians, not just consecrated celibates, in such statements as, "The man who tries to save his own life will lose it; it is the man who loses it that will keep it safe" (Luke 17.33); and, "Those who belong to Christ have crucified nature, with all its passions, all its impulses" (Gal. 5.24).

It is necessary to make clear that a broken heart is not always the same as a crucified or martyred heart. Christ's heart was both broken and martyred, but ours can be one or the other, or both, according to our interior dispositions.

We all know the kinds of human situations that lead to what we call heartbreak. "Here, O God, is my sacrifice, a broken spirit; a heart that is broken and contrite, thou, O God, wilt never disdain" (Ps. 50), can be interpreted to mean a human heart that, in the acutest forms of its suffering, does not recoil in anger, bitterness and self-pity, but gives itself to God in a faith and trust in divine providence that is often truly heroic. Thus the suffering of a broken heart can be made creative.

But a martyred heart is more than this. It is one that has undergone the extremes of suffering for the sake of the kingdom of heaven, or, to put it another way, the anguish of the heart has come essentially through its putting Christ always and unreservedly first. This has meant being crucified in its affective powers, since it has had to cooperate ruthlessly with grace in its work of transforming its "base human will" into "a divine will, being made one with the will of God."

To talk of crucifixion or martyrdom of the heart sounds extreme and frightening. Yet St. Paul's constant reiteration that we have to be crucified with Christ in order to be born anew and rise with him, following after our Lord's unequivocal warnings that we must take up our cross daily and follow him, make it plain that this is meant to be the normal, not the abnormal, way for all Christians. It seems abnormal in the twentieth century because ours is no longer an age of faith, but one where materialism prevails, and to say with St. Paul, "For me to live is Christ," is to invite the charge of fanaticism, or, what is even worse, to be merely boring.

Yet, the spiritual, eternal truth remains, that it was

Christ's passion, death and resurrection that saved the world. He summons us all to take a share in it, generously and to the point of laying down our lives in interior or exterior martyrdom, for the sake of one another.

If I were to outline a program likely to lead to this complete fitting into the pattern of his death and resurrection, it would go like this:

1. The essential, initial step must be the gift of the whole self to God without any reservations whatever, and the binding of the will to his, at whatever cost to oneself. Until this is done, the spiritual life cannot even really begin. Of course, as we progress in love, we realize how incomplete our gift of self and will has been, but the important thing is to make, and remake, this gift with all the sincerity and completion at our command at the time of giving. As later insights reveal imperfections, we resolve them by making the more complete oblation according to the new light given.

2. There must be a clear realization that the seat of the spiritual life is in the will, not the emotions. To speak of giving the heart suggests an emotional love, but the reality is the binding of the will and the continued effort and determination, against all odds, to keep that will faithful. The constant practice of self-abandonment to divine providence ensures this faithfulness, and the end aim is to become like putty in God's hands, till we say, "Yes, Lord," to every-

thing he does, wants, demands, lets happen, sends, inflicts and ordains, and never refuse him anything he asks.

3. This means deliberate, incessant, vigilant living to do everything to please him and nothing to offend him, and this will be mainly in very ordinary, unobtrusive and often boring ways connected with the faithful carrying out of whatever happen to be the duties of our state of life.

4. Since Christ is the way, the truth and the life, we must cultivate an intense personal relationship with him as a real person whose love desires complete union between himself and each one of us individually. Prayer, meditation, the sacraments, reading, and the effort to do everything in union with him and out of love for him are the main ways of cultivating this personal relationship.

5. This love union with Christ inevitably leads to the desire to take part in his redemptive act through creative suffering. The greater the love, the greater the generosity in this participation, until the cross seems branded into our lives, but in a way that leads to spiritual joy and liberation of the heart, never to gloom, pessimism and self-absorption.

6. Love of our neighbor, with no exceptions, is inseparable from love of Christ, and must be consciously cultivated all the time. This is obviously going to "crucify nature" for it is not the natural, spontaneous love of the amiable, gregarious tempera-

ment that is meant, but that supernatural, indiscrim-
inate, disinterested caring about others that is impossible without grace and hard work, and has
nothing to do with natural attraction or repulsion.

If such a program is persisted in sincerely for many
years, and no withdrawal of the total gift of self is
made, and no compromise sought, grace will work
that kind of miracle in our inner beings which is lived
out by our Lord in his resurrection from the dead. If
such a program is sealed by deliberate consecrations
(such as that of one's own heart to Christ) that are
peculiarly meaningful to oneself, and arise out of the
promptings of the Holy Spirit, then these will impact
an extra firmness and completeness to the total gift
of self.

The religious vocation, of course, has its own
traditional vows and consecrations, but those who
must live in the world are also called by God in ways
that fit in with the individual bent of our own
personal spirituality and temperament, to make
pledges with him. We have to be on the alert to the
Holy Spirit here, and always say yes to whatever he is
asking.

By such a program we learn to follow Christ to
Calvary, to mount the cross with him, to have our
hearts pierced with his, to be entombed with him,
and finally to rise to a new kind of existence in him.

6

SECRET IMMOLATION

WE tend to think that taking part in our Lord's passion with him through the purification of the heart will entail great and dramatic acts. On the contrary, it usually means a multitude of hidden, ordinary, tiny sacrifices carried on vigilantly, faithfully and humbly minute by minute as we go about our daily living and duties. As St. Thérèse said and exemplified, "Always doing the little things perfectly, and doing them for love."

There are few heroics in the spiritual life and the best immolation is a secret and hidden one. Very little is known of our Lady, and yet she was co-redemptress with her Son.

St. Thérèse's "little way" is open to all, and is by far the safe one to follow, since it is a way of humility and unobtrusiveness that protects us from the danger of being praised for "the great sacrifices we make for God." St. Francis de Sales said, "As a general rule extraordinary actions are done with less charity than ordinary ones."

The whole of the spiritual life centers on doing the will of God perfectly. Jesus in Gethsemane made to God's will that perfect submission out of perfect love that every Christian is bound to strive for. The incarnation began with such an act of the will when our Lady said, "Be it done to me according to your word." It continued in him who said openly, "My meat is to do the will of him who sent me. . . . It is the will of him who sent me, not my own will, that I have come down from heaven to do. . . . Father, if it be possible, let this cup pass from me. Nevertheless, not my will, but yours, be done."

Out of such submission to the mysterious plans of divine providence came the obedience which led to the cross, the salvation of the world, and the resurrection into heavenly life for all who follow him.

"Son of God though he was, he learned obedience in the school of suffering, and now, his full achievement reached, he wins eternal salvation for all those who render obedience to him" (Heb. 5.8-9).

Jesus expected us to follow his example of perfect conformity with God's will. He said, "If anyone does the will of my Father who is in heaven, he is my brother, and sister and mother" (Matt. 12.50). And, "The man who loves me is the man who keeps the commandments he has from me; and he who loves me will win my Father's love, and I too will love him, and will reveal myself to him" (John 14.21).

It sounds so simple, and yet for fallen man's disoriented nature, it is surpassingly difficult. That is why our Lord let himself endure Gethsemane, that we in our violent struggles for submission might know our Master is one "like us in all things except sin." He gave us the pattern, the mold, that we might know what it is we have to conform with, and by our willed union with him, receive the grace and strength we need.

The whole purpose of conformity with God's will is to form Christ in us, but God cannot do this unless we trustingly cooperate with his action. Mary trusted God enough to let him act, and so Christ was formed in her from the flesh and blood of her own body. He cannot form Christ spiritually in us unless we too join in her fiat. This will not mean being able to understand what he is doing. Looking back after years, we may see the pattern, but at the time of being shaped, all is too often darkness and interior confusion (as in Gethsemane), and only faith gives us courage to submit.

If the whole purpose of the spiritual life is to attain perfect conformity with God's will, then it is of crucial importance to train our wills (rebellious and self-seeking because of our disordered natures) to love his will. The refinements of conformity go far beyond merely avoiding sin, to a purification of heart so extreme that everything in our lives is done and suffered for one motive only — love.

God himself is love. Christ is love incarnate. The Holy Ghost is the Spirit of Love itself. God's will for us is love — an eternal and all-embracing union of love between us and him, and among ourselves for each other. In this life we attain this union by doing his will for love of him, just as our Lord did.

[63]

This doing of his will has an active and a passive aspect. The active one is the performance, for love, of all the duties that our particular way of life lays upon us, and the keeping of the commandments. The passive one is the reception, the embracement, for love, of all that God sends us, or permits to come to us, through the action of his providence in the circumstances of our lives, interior and exterior.

God presents himself to us, moment by moment, in the ordinary circumstances of our lives by what is called his "will of good pleasure" — what he lets happen. This is his divine providence in action. The sin-suffering-evil syndrome makes it hard for us to discern divine providence in action thus, but this is why we have faith. As Caussade says, "The life of faith is nothing but the continual pursuit of God through everything that disguises, disfigures, destroys, and, so to say, annihilates him. . . . All we have to do is receive what we are given and allow ourselves to be acted upon."[1]

It is not always easy to receive love. Usually we think of loving as giving, but it is also receiving others' love, often when we feel as if we do not want it. To receive God's love expressed for each of us in the ordinary circumstances of our individual lives, and to receive it with the wide embrace of Christ's arms spread on the cross, needs a lifetime's training and self discipline. As Caussade also says, "The art of self-abandonment is nothing but the art of loving," with emphasis on the art of receptivity. This means saying, "Yes, Lord. Thank you, Lord. Certainly, Lord," when all our natural impulse is to repudiate in utter distaste what God is offering.

The virtue of self-abandonment to divine providence, then, like any other virtue, has to be cultivated by means of deliberate effort and discipline. It is an axiom of the spiritual life that concentrating on any one virtue means that all the others are automatically developed too.

We begin with what God gives us day by day. It is best to begin practicing in small ways by accepting cheerfully, without irritation, fuss, impatience or complaint, all the minor frustrations, disappointments and pains that come along. The weather is a good one to start with, since there is precisely nothing we can do about it.

Then there are a multitude of opportunities in such things as being kept waiting for an appointment, missing a bus, the washing of clothes, getting wet, the car breaking down, developing an unsightly pimple, being unable to get a seat at the play, noisy neighbors at night, any one of our machines refusing to go, slugs eating the lettuces just planted, stubbing our toe, mud on the just-polished kitchen floor — there is endless variety. Whether man, woman, teenager or child, opportunity is never lacking here for discipline in self-abandonment.

In the process virtues such as patience, forbearance

and equanimity are strengthened.

Having developed some kind of control in these minor trials, it is time to go on to ones that are rather more serious. Such matters come to mind as one's children's failures and mistakes in things that really matter; hurtful actions and remarks by beloved friends we trusted; being publicly blamed and humiliated over some triviality when one is innocent; a setback at work that is going to affect one's future; the destruction of some precious and necessary property; a trying relative or friend to be cared for; the thwarting of important plans by illness or accident or some unforeseen event; sickness of a serious but not dangerous type; failure in some quite big enterprise. . . . Here there are more opportunities for virtues like humility, meekness, charity, trust detachment.

And so we are led into the practice of abandonment in regard to those matters which really reach our inner beings. These are different for each person, yet some such things as these are likely to be the material God gives us to work on — serious and painful illness, even perhaps a terminal disease and sentence of death; complete defeat of plans, work or projects which we have undertaken in obedience to God himself; humiliation and misjudgment over serious issues when we are quite innocent; temptations of unusual ferocity; interior desolation that is prolonged and intense; the loss of those especially dear and particularly of those who seem necessary for our spiritual growth; great suffering in those we love most and in a way that defies our help and consolation to them; some humiliating affliction, setback or handicap that seems to reduce us to uselessness to God and man. . . .

When such severe and searching trials come, the opportunities for secret immolation are endless and the self-discipline involved can reach heroic levels as faith, hope and charity come to perfection.

Comparatively few are asked to undertake the obviously great enterprises for God, but all are called to secret immolation, and opportunities for it are never lacking. But though the opportunities are so numerous, recognition of them is not so common. By various defense mechanisms we constantly shield ourselves from awareness so that we can excuse ourselves from making the hidden sacrifice of self.

What are some other practical ways in which we can develop self abandonment and attain secret immolation?

One is the Amen prayer. The word "Amen" means "May it be so." When we say Amen at the end of a prayer we are underlining everything we have said, or putting it in imaginary italics, or saying, "Now please take notice of that, Lord, because I mean what I say."

Our Lady's fiat was an Amen uttered for her whole life, and for every single thing that God chose to send her in it, including the crucifixion of her Son. It was renewed with every breath, every heartbeat, till her death.

Our Lord's life was one perpetual Amen, uttered in the exaltation and perfect submission of pure love. To the divine-human Amen of Jesus was added the totally human one of Mary, and from these combined Amens evolved the redemption of the human race.

Amen, then, is not just a word to say automatically at the end of a prayer, before we scramble hurriedly out of the pew to attend to more important matters. No — it is a state of being, a way of living, a means of union with Christ.

Learning to say it properly means learning the lesson of obedience from primary to university level. The saints, of course, occupy professorial chairs, but they never make any fuss about it, and most of the time no one but God knows they are there. They hide their expert proficiency beneath humility, which is one of the loveliest ways of all of saying Amen.

The Amen of humility is constantly telling God that we are pleased with where he has put us, in the lowest place at the feast, because we know quite well it is where we really belong. It is always blessing God for all his glory, and forgetting to notice ourselves. It is always accepting gratefully whatever God sends, out of a huge trust that he knows best what to do for our growth in love, and all our welfare, spiritual and temporal. It is always thanking him for his graces and asking for more, in a spirit of peaceful beggary.

The Amen of humility has very little to say to God except the cry of adoration and obedience, "My Lord and my God! Do whatever you like with me, I belong to you."

It does not puff itself up with wordy demands for this and that, with reproaches and complaints, with fearful expectations of the worst, with outpourings of misery. It does not need to do these things, for it is serenely at peace in God's will. It knows that he has filled the hungry with good things, and will continue to do so, and it knows also that it is one of the hungry, and that therefore all it has to do is wait in love, and accept in peace.

The fruit of learning to say Amen properly is, above all, peace. Our Lord said Amen through his whole life, but his supreme utterance was in Gethsemane. The next day the Amen of the garden was continued on the cross. "Into your hands I commend my spirit," and, "It is consumated."

What more beautiful way of saying Amen is there than to tell God, "Into your hands I commend my spirit, and all my affairs and my whole life?" Having done that night and morning, we may sleep tranquilly and pass undisturbed through the day's happenings, content to say Amen in our hearts to each of them. Even if they lead to crucifixion and death our answer can still be Amen.

This is the prayer of perfect peace, that peace

which the world is quite incapable of giving, but which Christ promised to those who love him and share his passion with him.

Prayer can be simplified into one long, usually wordless Amen. It becomes a disposition of the heart, a direction of the will, and it molds the soul into the likeness of Christ. Many people cannot get through the day without a drug called, ironically, a tranquilizer — but those who have learned to say the Amen prayer perfectly have no need of such artificial aids to serenity. They possess it always in the depths of their souls, and it makes them incapable of dismay or terror, no matter what happens.

They say with the psalmist, "Blessed be the Lord God of Israel, who does wonderful deeds as none else, and blessed for ever be his glorious name; all the earth shall be filled with his glory. Amen. Amen" (Ps. 71).

The Amen prayer leads to a spreading out of our while lives into the presence of God, a decrease of self and an increase of Christ, a leaning against the heart of Mary which with every beat says, "Blessed be God. Amen, Amen."

It leads to union, second by second, with the great Amen of the liturgy, being offered up all over the world at the Mass. This Amen occurs at the end of the canon, just before the Our Father, and it indicates our approval of all that God has done for us, of the offering up of our Lord in loving sacrifice for us, and of the joining of ourselves to him in that offering. It says, "May all these things be so for ever and ever, and may I be a part of them for all eternity."

It agrees to the total gift of ourselves to God. It accepts the consequences of that gift. It affirms that all that God does is good and that everything works together for good in the lives and souls of those that love the Lord. This great Amen of the Church is meant to be echoed constantly in the life, heart and will of every member of the mystical body. It is the flowing up of humanity to God, and it brings down the abundance of his love and graces upon the world.

St. Francis de Sales expressed his Amen in these words: "I desire nothing, I ask nothing, I refuse nothing." Such passivity under God's action is a good counter to today's fashionable over-activity for its own sake. Such submission means becoming a kind of sorting center for divine influences and graces that God wants extended to others, but which they are refusing to accept because they want to be self-sufficient. The abandoned person becomes the necessary human intermediary in such cases, in the mysterious workings of grace.

Allied to the Amen prayer is the refusal to make plans for God. Jesus said, "Your heavenly Father knows well what your needs are before you ask him" (Matt. 6.8), and, "Make it your first care to find the kingdom of God, and his approval, and all these things shall be yours without the asking. Do not fret, then, over tomorrow. Leave tomorrow to fret over its

[71]

own needs. For today, today's troubles are enough" (Matt. 6.33-34).

Anxiety is caused by lack of abandonment, by fear that God cannot be trusted to plan his universe and will end up – or begin – by doing the wrong thing if we do not guide and correct him. It screws itself up into the tension of dread that the worst is going to happen while God is looking the other way. It is in a perpetual "fret over tomorrow" and forgets all about seeking the kingdom of God in the present moment, while it feverishly chases an ephemeral security based in humans and in the things of this world.

Those who insist on making plans for God imagine that all he has to do is give substance and reality to their imagination and present them with the finished product. If he does not comply, they become peevish, sour, bitter, resentful, and may even decide to pay him back by not praying any more, or leaving the Church, or ceasing to believe in him.

They interpret very literally, and to their own material advantage, the injunction, "Ask and you shall receive." They do not seem to realize that God is the omnipotent and all-holy Father, and that they themselves may well be in the spiritual position of the toddler reaching for the glittering, fascinating carving knife, and having a temper tantrum when it is removed from his reach.

On the other hand, those who have faith in the Architect of the universe, who made the Milky Way and the daisy on the back lawn, the whale shark and the mouse, know that his ideas are bound to have more scope than theirs. His solution to problems is fairly certain to be wiser and more comprehensive than anything they can think up. Consequently, they are glad to enter into the secret immolation of turning over their whole lives to him. They are glad to sacrifice their own grandiose schemes and clever, long term plans in favor of letting him work out his own schemes and plans without their interference.

Through this immolation of self-will and self-seeking they learn the art of waiting on God. They crucify their natural impatience to get things done, see results, achieve, measure, count and multiply. From the cultivation of the art of waiting until Perfect Wisdom chooses for them, their motives are purified, and a holy indifference, a blessed detachment, gradually develops in their hearts.

They learn not to go on clutching when God says, "Let go," not to grab when they want something, but to wait until he puts it into their calm, relaxed hands. St. Thérèse said, "Sanctity does not consist in performing such and such acts; it means being ready at heart to become small and humble in the arms of God, acknowledging our own weakness, and trusting in his fatherly goodness to the point of audacity," and, "It is a source of such peace to be utterly poor, to count on nothing but the love of God."[2]

This inward poverty and weakness, this ability "to

glory in our infirmities," arises from the secret immolation of the desire to acquire merit, to keep a graph on the state of our growing sanctity, to make profit and loss accounts with God, to engage in that kind of celestial arithmetic that leads to priding ourselves on our own virtues.

Secret immolation means that, as well as turning over our whole lives to God, we turn over to him also the use of all graces and merits we receive from him. "Everything I have I give away immediately to buy souls," said St. Thérèse. "Merit does not arise from performing great deads or giving much, but in receiving and loving."[3]

The poor and weak need God. The rich and strong think they can manage without him. God gives himself in response to our need, not in response to our jealously guarded and minutely assessed merits and virtues. Secret immolation ruthlessly jettisons all these, knowing that virtue and merit belong to Christ alone and that his strength is made perfect in our weakness. "Seeing yourself so worthless you wish no longer to look at yourself, you look only at the sole Beloved."[4]

In the way of secret immolation we do not choose our own penances, but instead train ourselves to accept lovingly the penances sent by God. No day is flawless, and some days are almost unbearable. That is to say, every day carries its load of penance, even though it be only a sackload of pinpricks, and so every day is given us by God as a means of making up for our own sins and those of others. But half the time we are engaged in pushing away his penances as soon as they present themselves.

The alarm rings. We sleepily switch it off and turn over for another comfortable little doze. To do penance would be to get up immediately.

Someone rebukes us, and, ruffled, we indignantly or self-righteously justify ourselves. A valuable opportunity for practicing humility is lost-penance offered by God, and refused by us.

We see an intolerable bore approaching, and hastily cross the street before she catches sight of us, or we clap eyes on someone we had a tiff with a year ago, and quickly avert our gaze lest we should be obliged to stop and speak pleasantly: treasured chances to do violence to self-love thrown away; opportunities for practicing charity disregarded; chance to forgive trespasses squandered; penance offered by God, refused by us.

We have a cold in the head, or a pain in the back, or a bunion, or indigestion, or a headache, or an itchy rash — and we waste it all by grizzling and looking for sympathy to anyone who happens to come near, and indulging in foam-rubber cushions of self-pity when we are alone: penance offered by God, refused by us.

We miss the bus. We make a mistake about the time of a favorite TV program. The children are incredibly trying. It comes on to rain just when we are going to tennis. We get a puncture half way to work. Someone carelessly scratches the paint on the new car. We can't find the screwdriver. . . .

A series of irritating small happenings, and we waste them all, for instead of using them as opportunities for practicing patience, meekness, forbearance, and exercising our sense of humor, we give way to temper, grouse to ourselves and anyone handy, make testy suggestions that everyone is deliberately trying to annoy us, and fume and fret till we are most unpleasant to be near. Penance offered by God, and refused by us.

We have set our hearts on getting a certain job, passing a certain examination, winning a certain prize, being elected chairman to that committee, gaining a certain person's friendship, succeeding in a certain enterprise . . . and all our hopes are confounded. We give way to depression and anger, we feel slighted and indulge our feelings. No one appreciates us at our true worth, we assure ourselves. We deserve better than this, and why haven't we got it? We complain bitterly.

Precious chance to practice utter abandonment to God lost. Invaluable opportunity to remind ourselves that we should be laying up treasure in heaven rather than upon earth, thrown away. First class opening to practice serene trust in God, to accept his will rather than our own, to mortify attachment to worldly recognition, carelessly passed by.

[76]

Penance offered by God, and refused by us.

And so it goes on. The opportunities are God-sent, and we either remain quite oblivious of them, or else wilfully refuse to cooperate with his plans for us because we are piqued that they are different from our plans for ourselves.

If we could train ourselves to say to every disappointment, trial, pain, frustration, setback, no matter how small: "This is the penance that God sends, therefore it is the best possible penance for me," and to embrace it cheerfully and lovingly, then we would really be doing something for God's kingdom.

7

THE TYRANNY OF DESIRES

ONE of the basic tenets of the spiritual life is that grace perfects nature.

God made all things and pronounced them good, including the human heart, but it was this very heart that chose to go "whoring after strange gods" and desiring fulfillment in ways other than those ordained by God. The heart as God made it was meant to be the repository of his love poured uninterruptedly into it. It was as uninterruptedly to respond to this love with the total gift of self.

But much has happened to this plan of God for the happiness and fulfillment of our hearts. We have become "mixed up" in much the same way as today's "mixed up" adolescent who more or less runs amok.

Our hearts have run amok. They are out of control. They do not desire God but the things that God has created, that is, instead of being led by the Spirit, they are led by their senses. They have lost the sense of proportion that kept right relations among things. They have set up a multitude of idols, and like the Israelites have forgotten God's ancient command, "You shall have no other gods but me . . . for I am a jealous God."

It is our nature to love – but it is also our nature

to love perversely. The heart has to be re-educated and renewed, and it is in this very process that grace perfects nature.

"At eventide they will examine thee in love. Learn to love as God desires to be loved, and lay aside thine own temperament."[1]

This is a summary of the program. It is not our own selfish desires that must be satisfied, but God's desires. He wants to be loved, and in a certain way which will bring harmony and hierarchical pattern into our hearts. But to go his way instead of our own will mean the pain and self-denial of "laying aside our own temperaments," our own pressing psychological needs, our own emotional cravings, our own self-centered desires, our own convictions about what is good for us. He may well make use of these as his grace perfects our nature, but it is for him, not us, to decide which of them shall be fulfilled and which annihilated.

The fallen heart manifests its self-love and self-will through the strength, variety and perversity of its desires. It is continually crying "I want!" like a fledgling with its mouth wide open, squawking to be filled. It is very far from the peace and composure that comes with that purity of intention that wants only God and his will.

It is not desire itself that is wrong, but the misdirection of desire. Because of our innate tendency to misdirect, all desires except that to love God

[79]

and do his will, are suspect. They are all tainted with self-love and self-will. They all want to build up our own egos, rather than make them less and less so that Christ may be more and more in us.

We tell ourselves that unless we can possess what or whom we desire, we cannot be complete as human beings, or discover our true identity and role. We rationalize about the desired object until we find excuses to make it an extension of ourselves so that we can experience fulfillment, pleasure and satisfaction through it.

There is never a thought in all this of directing desire so that it is functioning only for the honor and glory of God. Rather, we are compulsively seeking honor and glory for ourselves.

The purification of the heart is concerned with re-establishing right order and a sense of proportion. The will has to be trained to maintain unswervingly its direction towards God. It has to practice putting God first. In order to do this, it will often have to mortify desires and go without fulfillments for which the heart is clamoring. It has to recognize its own tendency to misdirection and be on the watch to eliminate or modify all desires and practices that can aggravate this tendency, or induce "mixedupness."

This does not mean slaughtering the heart, but keeping its impulses and affections heading in the direction God wants them — towards himself, while going on trying to love as he wants it to love — selflessly.

It means striving towards what St. Augustine called "the tranquillity of right order," the peace of living in conformity with God's will. It means disciplining our wills to "hunger and thirst after righteousness" and the kingdom of heaven within, rather than crave for "the world" that Jesus warned against. It means being on guard about immersion in pleasure for its own sake and in the intoxication of attaining our desires and possessing what or whom we have craved. It means repudiating what used to be called "inordinate affections."

It is impossible to follow this re-education program without a conscious cultivation of the presence of Christ within our hearts, and a humble drawing on his strength in our efforts to maintain a true perspective and make the right choices. Where he is strongly present, worldly desires lose some of their imperiousness and it becomes possible to do without what we thought was absolutely necessary to us.

This program of controlling, redirecting or eliminating desires will go on for decades. All those cravings that have power to deflect us from aiming straight at God, and finally lead us into sin if we recklessly indulge them, have to be mortified.

Since God made us for himself, it is obvious that if our interior being is in "the tranquility of right order" it will be ruled by one supreme desire to attain love union with God.

St. John of the Cross warns that desires other than those "to keep the law of God perfectly, and to bear upon oneself the cross of Christ" can bring to one who fosters them the loss of the Spirit of God, together with weariness, torment, darkness, defilement and weakness.[2] That is, they lead to the opposite state from the tranquility of right order, and to severance from Christ.

If we say, "I know what I want. I'm going to have it and no one's going to stop me — not even God," we are losing the Spirit of God because we are driving him out by our wilfullness. We set our hearts on what is finite and temporal, instead of on the infinite and eternal for which God made them. Consequently, we invite weariness, torment and the rest, because of our very nature we cannot be satisfied by what we crave. Possession of it will not bring the fulfillment we imagine, whatever the temporary easing of stress.

The results of directing what is really man's inescapable hunger for God to desires for the temporal and material can be seen in our Western way of life. Most of the curses of the modern world originate in this misdirection of desire, and its accompanying fever for possession. Our disquiet, our restlessness, our craze for speed, change and new sensations, are very different from that divine discontent which is the lack of satisfaction in all things except God, the longing to possess God himself, and be possessed by him.

Every desire that is not secondary to this desire for God himself is an expression of our fallen heart's waywardness. The more they are indulged, the further we move away from God, until perhaps we finally deny him entry altogether, and are lost to our only chance of true peace.

It is obvious that we cannot live in the world without possessions and without the usage of material things, including money. The danger is not in possessions, but in possessiveness. It lies in valuing and wanting things for their own sakes and because they enhance our self-opinion and feed our self-interest.

The solution is in using and possessing things while mortifying that anxious sense of ownership, and in awareness that God created and owns all things, including ourselves. We are only stewards, and unprofitable ones at that.

When desire for ownership is directed towards human beings rather than material things, peace of mind and heart are placed even more in jeopardy. We have handed ourselves over, bound to a creature as fickle and capricious as ourselves, making our hearts captive, instead of freeing them for God.

No human being is reliable to the perfect degree our hearts needs. None is to be trusted as God intends us to trust him. All are finite and corruptible, yet we may never learn properly the lesson that to want to say "mine" over any of them is to invite torment, not joy. It is to hand ourselves over to emotional enslavement instead of to the peace and release God offers us.

If we let our desires rule us, instead of we them, we automatically lower our status as human beings. Our wills have become bound by the force of these unchecked cravings, and in our inner darkness and storm we cannot feel the calm promptings of Wisdom, or sit still and pay attention to God.

Strong desires are forces of great energy, potentially destructive if not directed to their one true end. When misdirected they can produce chaos, just as an earthquake or tornado does.

Such misdirection is a form of self-indulgence. "He denied not his heart that which it demanded of him."[3] It makes us prefer rationalizations to truth, because they supply us with excuses for our weaknesses rather than light on the damage being done. It blinds us to the fact that until we have mortified our cravings, we will not be free to see God's will, let alone do it. It tosses us into emotional disturbances centered around the urge to possess — "At last this is truly mine, and no can take it from me!"

Such possession does not elevate or ennoble. By our clinging, we fasten ourselves to the material and our craving to enjoy it, and are severed from the spiritual, our true end. Instead of fulfilling our function to be other Christs, we become adjuncts of the first syndrome, and repositories for its distorted values.

Misdirected desires shelter elements of self-interest and self-seeking that cause us to manipulate and make use of others, to indulge in deviousness and meanness in order to get our own way. Our memory and imagination play about with the images of what is desired, providing major distractions to a spirit of recollection. We become obsessed with certain ideas, memories, happenings, and build on them with false imagination till we make them into what we want them to be.

"All they do is lie to one another, flattering lips, talk from a double heart" (Ps. 12.2). We all indulge in this far more than we like to admit. And why? From a desire to be well thought of, a desire to curry favor, a desire to impress, a desire to arouse interest, a desire to humiliate others in order to enhance our own self-image.

Desires fasten us to the millstone of useless turning over and over of the past, wishing it were still here; or of imagining a future which we hope will eventuate. There is an inner feeding of substanceless suppositions that bleeds away our spiritual forces.

Since, in order to attain love union with God, the whole will and heart must be set on him, this sapping of strength is fatal. A divided will cannot be a strong, purposeful will.

8

CUSTODY OF THE HEART

WE cannot learn to love God as he wishes until we acknowledge that the heart (meaning all in us that yearns towards others and all our manifestations of that yearning) is willful and difficult to control. It is a fallen heart, the repository of passions and desires that clamor for satisfaction. It is tainted with self-interest and *amour propre*. It is deceitful and devious. It is the product of the first syndrome.

At the same time it is capable of noble devotion and sacrifice. It is fanatically loyal, and tender in the extreme. It pours out a healing, generous sympathy. It puts itself aside in acts of altruism. It adores and prostrates itself in humility before beauty, goodness and truth. It yearns towards the second syndrome.

With such an ambivalent force inside him, it is no wonder that man is often inconsistent and as often racked by indecision. Some ruling passion may lead him to devote his whole life to a person or cause, yet to be a Christian his ruling passion must be fixed on God, and the person or cause served for God's sake and because it is his will.

What St. Paul calls "the real circumcision of the heart, something not of the letter but of the spirit" (Rom. 2.29) cannot take place without custody of the heart, which is really what St. John of the Cross has explained in his exposition of the danger of desires in *Ascent III.* Like most other aspects of Christian living, this entails a paradox. We have to keep control over our heart, yet we must not frighten or cudgel it into being a caged heart.

A false idea about its custody might lead to such a fear of loving in the wrong way, that the heart might lock itself up in a dungeon, or be locked up by our own dread of excess or mismanagement.

Right loving is inseparable from fear of God, but this should be the kind of fear we have of hurting someone inexpressibly dear to us. It is at least partially true to say that many will never learn the right way to fear God until they know what it is to fear hurting some greatly loved human being. God is a Person, not an abstract or an absolute. He became incarnate, and what we do to him and to each other, we do to Jesus.

We cannot love our Lord with a caged heart.

A caged heart is ruled by dread. It has sometimes atrophied into a withered kernel that has no warmth and spontaneity left; and it has sometimes turned into an imprisoned animal, savage and impatient, pacing the cage and glaring through the bars, increasing our dread of what might happen were we to give it even a taste of what it craves.

It can be very dangerous not to love.

It can be equally dangerous to love.

[87]

Some people have a psychological quirk about loving and being loved. Motivated by obscure anxiety and guilt complexes, they protect their hearts by a system of Chinese boxes one inside the other. As each box is dissolved away by a mixture of grace and effort, the prisoner rejoices, crying out in thanksgiving and praise, "Now at last I'm free! I'm free!"

Before long, however, he comes hard up against the next barrier of the series, till finally he reaches those which can be dissolved only by mysteriously hidden workings of grace. These are the cages of the darkest, deepest places of the individual substrata, and their dissolution sometimes entails martyrdom of the heart for certain kinds of people.

Whatever the cage our self-protection system has devised, it is the wrong kind of custody of the heart if it is motivated by fear, self-interest, or pride, instead of the desire to love God perfectly.

We have to sort out, with the help of grace and pitiless honesty, what is appetite of one kind or another, and what is beginning to be true Christian love, that is, what is, at least to a marked degree, free of the need and desire for self-satisfaction.

"A man who hankers after ashes has a deluded heart and is led astray. He will never free his soul, or say, What I have in my hand is nothing but a lie" (Is. 44.20).

"This "hankering after ashes," after what belongs to space-time and will die when we do, what will have

no part in our eternal life, what is in no way a route
to God, what is not to his honor and glory, wears
countless disguises. We have often learnt to kiss the
bonds of our "hankering" with a ludicrous smugness,
giving them all kinds of high-sounding names in our
rationalizations.

Custody of the heart means training the heart not
to run after delusions, not to call ashes rose petals.
Often this can be done only in the field of action,
that is, only in situations where we are relating to
people warmly and personally.

We learn to control immoderate or perverted tastes
for food not by starving ourselves, but by training the
palate to like what is good for us, and our appetite to
be satisfied with moderation. Similarly we learn
custody of the heart not by caging it or putting it in
deep-freeze, but by exercising our innate need to love
and be loved in a moderate manner and in ways that
reason tells us, and prayer reveals to us, are good.

We are not alcoholics whose only remedy is to
abstain from alcohol altogether, though a Jansenist
view of human nature would have us believe so. We
have been baptized into Christ, have his life in us, and
have been told to love as he loves. Doing this requires
a combination of self-discipline and training (all that
the *Ascent* has to say about desires), coupled with the
continual growth of grace in our hearts, until they are
wholly possessed by Christ.

There are few saints who have been warmer and

more loving in their personal relationships that St. Teresa of Avila. There was never a time in her life when she was not most affectionately involved with numbers of people. But there did occur a plain turning point after some eighteen years of what she herself frankly admits was spiritual tepidity. During these years, and in spite of great struggles, she could not renounce the satisfaction and pleasure that human loving gave her. She ran to the parlor because she loved to be liked and appreciated. Her warm heart and volatile temperament basked in affection given and received. She enjoyed conversation and the exchange of confidences and the stimulation of company.

There was nothing really sinful in any of this, since it was not contrary to either rule or custom. In fact, many people would label such outgoingness, vivacity and warmth, virtues. But Teresa knew in her heart that it "came to the same thing whether a bird be held by a slender cord or by a stout one,"[1] and she also knew she was held.

Finally she was able to cut the thread under the guidance of a certain priest.

"This Father began to lead me to greater perfection. He told me that I ought to leave nothing undone so as to become entirely pleasing to God, and he treated me with great skill, yet also very gently, for my soul was not at all strong, but very sensitive, especially as regards abandoning certain friendships which were not actually leading me to offend God. There was a great deal of affection beneath these and it seemed to me that if I abandoned them I should be sinning through ingratitude; so I asked him why it was necessary for me to be ungrateful if I was not offending God. He told me to commend the matter to God for a few days, and to recite the hymn *Veni, Creator,* and I should be enlightened as to which was the better thing to do."[2]

She did as she was told, and the turning point came.

In a rapture, her first, it seemed to her that God told her that now he wanted her "to converse not with men, but with angels." She records that from the moment she had the grace of complete custody of the heart.

"Never since then have I been able to maintain firm friendship save with people who I believe love God and try to serve him, nor have I derived comfort from any others or cherished any private affection for them. It has not been in my own power to do so; and it has made no difference if the people have been relatives or friends. Unless I know that a person loves God and practices prayer, it is a real cross to me to have to do with him."[3]

That all her efforts in previous years had not enabled her to attain custody of the heart, and that she had to wait till God gave it as a gratuitous grace, taught her humility. Until the end of her life she loved ardently and simply those who were close to her in Christ. In her last years she was exceedingly devoted to Father Gracian, and she died in the arms of her beloved Ana of St. Bartholomew.

She remained human with a human heart, yet a heart so taken over by Christ that its loving was transformed into his loving – free of self-interest, compulsion, appetite and unrest.

Never dehumanized, she is an excellent example of the right kind of custody of the heart.

For custody of the heart does not mean its destruction, but its training. It is emptied out of self so it may be filled with God – but God is never apart from human beings, and the first commandment is inseparable from the second. We go on loving, but all our loving is an effort to love rightly. We do not relax vigilance for one moment, and whatever God indicates must be given up, we renounce immediately not from fear, but for love of him.

An analogy between the Christian seeking God and a married couple may be drawn.

The married couple have vowed the complete gift of themselves to each other for life. This can be compared to the Christian's baptismal and confirmation promises.

After marriage, each is free to love others as long as the marriage partner is always put first. Similarly the Christian is free to, in fact must, love others, but always with God put first.

Our baptism initiates a marriage union with Christ,

with the Trinity, to which we must be faithful. It is fulfilled and perfected in the heights of the spiritual marriage, which St. John of the Cross points out is essentially the complete fusion of the human will (heart) with the divine will (see *Ascent,* P. 49). This spiritual marriage may or may not be accompanied by extraordinary mystical graces. If so, they are the accidents, not the substance, of the union. The substance is always in the will.

"The soul cannot reach this equality and completeness of love save by the total transformation of the will in that of God, wherein the two wills are united after such a manner that they become one."[4]

Custody of the heart is the same as custody of the will. It is perfect when, like our Lord, we desire only to do God's will because it is the spiritual equivalent of "meat and drink" to us.

What St. John of the Cross has to say about "the affection of love" will throw light on what is meant by custody of the heart.

He uses the term to mean an emotion or drive that includes a desire to possess. He speaks of the "four passions of joy, hope, fear and grief," but he also calls these "affections" (cf. *Ascent III,* P. 244). He uses the same word in conjunction with "inclination" and "attachments" (P. 241).

There is a direct connection here with all that he teaches about misplaced and immoderate desires. To have an "affection" for something means to set one's heart upon it in order to possess it. "If we had to

[93]

describe the evils which encompass the soul when it sets the affections of its will upon temporal blessings, neither ink nor paper would suffice."[5]

Such "creature affection" invites spiritual disaster, whereas "the soul that is united with God by the affection of its will enjoys all blessings."[6] "Absorption in this joy of creatures" is so dangerous that he warns, "For, if a man is to be perfectly defended from the affection of love, he must preserve an abhorrence of it."[7]

To the strength of this prohibition must be added his statement that God looks "with affection of love" on the soul that is united with him in the spiritual marriage.[8] Hence it is plain that the affection of love can be rightly or wrongly directed, and when St. John advocates an abhorrence of it he means to be understood (as with desires) "when it is being misdirected."

E. W. Trueman Dicken writes, " 'Passions' and 'affections' between them include most of the functions attributed in modern parlance to the emotions. The concept of emotion in fact finds no place in Scholastic psychology."[9]

It is necessary to clarify this point, for "the affection of love" in modern usage would mean something wholly good — the tenderness and self-giving gentleness of a mother for her child, or a friend for a friend. This, of course, is not to be "abhorred" — far from it.

The abhorrence is necessary only when there is a desire to possess, a craving to have as one's own, for it is this that has power to drive a person to turn his back on God and to choose the creature instead of the Creator.

Most of what St. John has to say on this topic is included in *Ascent III* in those chapters which deal with the purgation of the will. The connection is clear when we remember that heart equals will.

The affection of love can be inflamed by a memory that deliberately dwells upon who or what is desired, and so it is important that the memory itself be purged and actively controlled. No feeding of fantasies, no romantic sighs, no abstracted gazes while the inward eye is absorbed in contemplating the desirability of the object that is hankered after.

In order to control the affection of love it is necessary to say "no" to those aspects of memory that compulsively return to the object desired. It is a help to practice a method of disidentification with the compulsion. Instead of thinking, "I desire . . . I want . . . I remember . . . I hope . . .," think, "Something in me . . . My unredeemed self . . ." or else make up some ironical name that will make fun on these hankerings — "Romantic Ronnie . . . Lovelorn Lisa . . . Obsessed Osbert. . . ."

St. Paul himself does something similar in the passage, Romans 8.14-25, where he speaks of "my unspiritual self" and "my true self."

The personality is never united until integrated in Christ, that is, in a state of spiritual marriage. Until then it is a multiplicity of warring I's, among which we have deliberately to choose to foster some, and to disidentify with others. Peace comes finally when all these I's are gathered in willing submission about the will of God that has become the focal point, the nucleus, of the whole personality. Recognition of this fact is a help in the control of desires.

The affection of love is innate in humans. If we are incapable of it, we are psychopaths. It is inseparable from our natural need to love and be loved, and can almost be equated with that yearning. Yet, because of the fall, original sin and the first syndrome, we have this fatal tendency to misdirect our affective powers. Hence the urgency of the need to discipline the affection of love.

Custody of the heart is this disciplining process. It is a constant, minute by minute, unrelaxed determination to choose God before choosing any love object from among those he has created. It is the resolve, no matter what it cost us in terms of loneliness, grief at separation, longing for loved companionship, to say "no" to the affection of love whenever it clamors to engulf us, to possess us rather than submit to our control. It is like Lear crying to his passions as to springing dogs, "Down, thou climbing sorrow! Thy element's below . . . O me! my heart, my rising heart! but, down!"[10]

9

SOME CHIEF ATTRIBUTES

"YOU have stripped off your old behavior with your old self, and you have put on a new self which will progress towards true knowledge the more it is renewed in the image of its creator" (Col. 3.9-10).

This combined "stripping off" and "putting on" occurs in a great variety of ways, according to the type of personality and character involved.

Hearts have different kinds of chief attributes on which the work of grace and of self-discipline must be centered. This chapter suggests a few of the main ones and gives some indication of ways in which purification might occur.

The Divided Heart. The natural state of any fallen heart is one of disorder and division. What was meant to be unified in the peace of doing and accepting God's will as the clearly recognized highest good, is instead often uncertain of its direction. Entry into the dark night means the heart wants to place Christ at its center, but in actual fact its attention is very often distracted and its force dissipated because it has yet to be purified.

It has not one "I" that is merged with the Christ-self established by grace within, but many "I's" clamoring for fulfillment and notice. They will all have to be severely disciplined, starved of attention and satisfaction, before integration and unity of purpose is attained.

Fragmentation of purpose, and distraction from the ideal chosen, are typical of the fallen heart, and much of the dark night will be concerned with recognizing these fragmentations and distractions and mortifying them.

The best way of unifying the divided heart is by deliberate cultivation of intimacy with Jesus present in the soul as its source of grace, its strength and its exemplar. Whatever seeks to stray from his presence has to be gently turned back to its true home. Whatever is unworthy, yet wants to remain in the Lord's presence, must be measured against his beauty, purity and holiness, and either purified or cast out if it withers before his glance.

He is the center, the nucleus, the growing point of the heart longing for renewal. When all the heart's warring elements are either cast out because unworthy of him, or incorporated into his divine life because made subject to it, division will cease, and integration be achieved.

The Restless Heart is inevitably part of the divided heart. As long as the heart persists in straying after idols instead of seeking its peace and fulfillment in Christ alone, it will be afflicted with restlessness. As long as it does not recognize that its only lasting peace can be the peace of God that passes all understanding, it will seek here and there, passing from one disillusionment to another, fidgetting and dissatisfied.

> That piecemeal peace is poor peace. What pure peace allows
> Alarms of wars, the daunting wars, the death of it?

wrote Gerard Manley Hopkins.

The constant hunger for new experiences, change, entertainment, novelty, moving about, meeting people, nibbling at this and that intellectual or emotional tidbit, are characteristics of the restless heart, to which God says, "Be still, and know that I am God."

All this has to be replaced by that calm movement into its own center, that closing of its door and retirement into its inner chamber to pray, which is the sign of restlessness disciplined into recollection.

The Hardened Heart. "If today you hear his voice, harden not your hearts" (Ps. 95).

One might think that a hardened heart would never reach the stage of entering the dark night. However, it is true that, coupled with the good will necessary for entering, can be many involuntary and partly voluntary resistances against both God's will and the action of his grace.

The heart is like a rough piece of timber or an unhewn lump of marble before the craftsman has shaped and smoothed it. Although it no longer consciously and deliberately says, "I will not serve," if often rejects what God sends, in spite of itself.

Through rigidity in clinging to self-love and self-will, it refuses to incorporate into its ideas about itself unpalatable truths that the Spirit is presenting to it. The same rigidity makes it complain, and even show bitterness or rebellion, at manifestations of God's will that bring grave humiliation to its self-love, and painful thwarting and defeat to its self-will.

It lacks flexibility. It has not yet become so pliable that it is like a softened, comfortable, shaped glove or shoe that God can put his hand or foot into and use for whatever purpose he chooses, with no resistance on its part.

The Greedy Heart has a marked tendency to possessiveness. Maybe emotional insecurity drives it to seek apparent safety in amassing belongings – not necessarily material ones.

It may be so greedy for love and reassurance as to its worth that it sets out to captivate one person after another, finding in the possession of homage, admiration, compliments, flattery, friendships, a sop to its niggling sense of never having enough.

Such a heart is closely allied with the mistrustful, anxious heart. It has to learn not to lay up treasures for itself on earth, where moth and rust destroy, but in the imperishable kingdom of heaven within, where the spiritual blessings of Christ's presence surpass any possible earthly riches, and the joys and satisfaction derived from them.

The greedy heart is a victim of the "I want" complex, and has to learn to unify all its wants under the single heading "I want God."

The Inferior, Insecure Heart may follow the same pattern, always seeking to impress and be praised; or the opposite one of doormat techniques, taking a perverse pleasure in feeding its darkest suspicions about itself by inviting humiliations, spurnings, disparagements. It may seek "the lowest place of all" to gratify hidden guilts and fears, and not from any genuine humility.

Such a heart has to learn, painfully and slowly, that its true worth is not to be found in any human judgments of it, but in God's love and mercy alone. It is nothing, and justly so, in his sight, and yet it is also chosen for the incredible grace of love union with him in the Son through the Spirit.

It has to learn, with St. Paul, not to boast except in its humiliations (and then only for Christ's sake), and in the cross of Christ. Like John the Baptist, it must discipline itself to rejoice in becoming less and less so that Christ in it can become more and more.

The Hungry Heart longs for love, and usually has a great capacity for love. Yet just because its potential is so great, it tends to go in the wrong direction, towards creatures, to satisfy it. It is aware of a void within it that aches to be filled, and because God seems to be taking so long to do his part, such a heart suffers severe temptations, to which it may succumb, to try to fill the void and appease the ache with human love.

All the time it must practice sublimation, and though the effort of lifting may cause it to groan, it must hold up to Christ, for his blessing and sanctifying, what it longs to cram into its void. It must exercise great faith and hope that one day, if it perseveres, God will indeed appease its hunger with what "eye has not seen" and fill it to completion with what "no mind has conceived."

The Lonely Heart is one that either has great difficulty in communicating or sharing, or else has so much to give that it can never find anyone adequate to receive it. It is often aware of being "different" and "set apart," though it cannot tell how and why. The painful overtures it makes to others in its efforts to achieve understanding and closeness, never or seldom seem to meet the kind of response it needs.

The lonely heart has often been administered such excruciating rebuffs that it has ceased reaching out at all, and maybe has tried to make a virtue of its loneliness by calling it "strength," or "self-sufficiency," or "detachment."

The lonely heart is a suffering heart and one that badly needs the experiential presence of Christ. Yet God may deny it this in order to purify its love of a selfish need for comfort.

It needs to discipline its tendency to introspection and self-pity, and sanctify its loneliness by uniting it with our Lord's in Gethsemane, in his passion, and on his cross. It must labor and pray for the grace to make its suffering redemptive with Christ's.

The Obsessed Heart has a ruling passion other than that to conform perfectly with God's will and love Jesus heroically. Again, goodwill has led it into the dark night, but it may well not stay there, or not persevere systematically, because of the strength of this one drive that amounts to a major distraction of mind, heart and will.

Whether this passion is the ambition to succeed in some work or career, or a concentration upon creative art, or a deviation that seems like a virtue to one person (a crippled child, an ailing parent, an alcoholic husband or friend), or anything else, it is misplaced.

The danger for such a heart is its tendency to rationalize about its obsession, to find excuses for it and label it "noble self-sacrifice," or "passionate search for truth," or the like. Some buried need is fed and satisfied by the indulgence of the obsession, and much painful work will have to be done by the Holy Spirit before right emphases are established.

Yet its mere capacity for such strength of application, even though it is misapplication, indicates that such a heart can love God mightily if only all its force can be turned in the right direction.

The Romantic Heart has a compulsive urge to put reality in fancy dress. It longs for the ideal, but transfers it from Christ to human beings or human causes. It has a strong tendency to idol worship, though this is not perverse and deliberate, but rather an involuntary deviation in sincere belief that what is adored is worthy.

Such a heart will suffer many bitter disillusionments before it really understands that God himself is the only right and proper object of worship. However, since by entering the dark night it has chosen truth and not illusion, God will give it the grace to persevere. It will learn to strip away the fancy dress in order to see the naked truth that all creatures derive whatever goodness, beauty and glory they have from their Creator.

The poetry it so passionately seeks in human relationships and created beauty will gradually recognize its true source. The heart will learn to aim straight at its divine target, Christ, finding the fulfillment for all its ardent dreams in him.

The Impotent Heart. Some hearts are, for psychological reasons beyond their control, strangely numb and inert in their responses. Sometimes this impotence renders them indifferent to God too, so that they never even enter the dark night. Sometimes it preserves them from passionate and distracting involvements on the human level, and so makes it easier for them to turn to God.

Sometimes a too easily aroused and responsive heart is, when it enters the dark night, made impotent by God himself in order to protect it and to wean it from delight in creatures.

Whatever the cause, the impotent heart will mourn its sterility and learn a very profound humility from it, if it does not rationalize about its affliction. Because it feels so incapable of human love, it must rely all the more on being supplied with divine love in order to fulfill the two commandments.

When it has reached intense anguish and self-contempt over its lack of love, God will take pity on it and pour into it all that it needs and craves.

If it has the courage to stay faithful and go on trying in spite of defeat after defeat, such a heart will in the end be Christ's true beloved.

The Distracted Heart is like Martha, fussing and worrying over too many matters, many of which are trivialities. It tends to rush around thinking love is proved by frantic action and a multitude of things actually done. It loses sight of the Lord in its preoccupation with endless duties and "deserving cases."

It is usually energetic, practical, pragmatic and unimaginative. It means well, but confuses priorities and loses proportion because the dust of its commotion is hiding the Lord from it.

Such a heart has great need to do violence to itself by deliberately practicing stillness. It has to learn to pause and take stock. In the silence, as the turmoil of its activity dies away, it must wait for the Spirit's gentle prompting. It has to mortify its constant urge to take the initiative from God, and understand that sometimes doing nothing (like Mary at the Lord's feet) can be the most powerful way possible of loving and praying.

The Hypersensitive Heart is hard to get on with. It is a bit like a sea anemone, withdrawing its slender, waving tentacles at the slightest touch into a tight ball of self-enclosure.

The hypersensitive heart is naturally thin-skinned, over-responsive and under-protected. It usually has a great capacity for love, but this is made almost incapable of expression by fear of being hurt. Introspection broods over hurt, magnifying it through false imagination, and sometimes provoking savage reprisal.

The hypersensitive heart tends to live in an unreal world, manufacturing slights where none was intended, imagining it is disliked when it has not even been noticed, indulging quite unnecessarily in the luxury of being hurt, being irritatingly touchy by twisting what is said to it or putting far-fetched derogatory interpretations on innocent remarks.

In fact, it is often a creative artist of the first order gone lamentably wrong.

Such a heart also has to learn proportion, and practice turning out instead of in. It has to discipline false imagination, mortify instead of indulge hurt feelings, and evolve its own methods of irony and humor about its own morbid sensitivities.

Its responsiveness is a valuable asset in its relations to the Holy Spirit, but it has to be stripped of its over-reaction pattern in human relations.

The Mistrustful, Anxious Heart does not know what it is to be reckless in loving. It fears to give its whole self to either God or human, and is always worrying about what might happen. It feels it must keep something in reserve in case of accidents, and finds it quite impossible to believe "sufficient unto the day is the evil thereof," and that God is taking care of every hair on everyone's head.

It wants to believe these things, but cannot. It has a real dread of letting God or humans into its secret self, and protective barriers are involuntary with it. It may see its condition quite clearly and feel real distress over it, but it will not be able to be different until grace does healing and renewing work in its buried life.

None of the above attributes of various hearts is of a malicious nature, for deliberately sinful hearts do not enter the dark night. Deliberate sin must be sincerely and persistently renounced, and good habits well established before a heart can develop enough hunger for God and clearsightedness to enable it to submit to purification.

Once in the night, some of the foregoing traits and imperfections, which are all symptomatic of man's fallen state, may well hinder its progress if not fully understood and countered.

10

THE IMPULSE TO ADORE — An
Elaboration on the Romantic Heart

WITHIN the complex of affective powers we call the heart, is an impulse to adore or worship. This impulse should rightly be directed towards God, for only he is perfect and worthy of man's adoration. But because man's heart is warped, the impulse becomes misdirected or deviated and turns into idolatry, or the worship of what God has made instead of God himself.

This adoration of the created is one aspect of romanticism which I wish to examine because it is a parody of the love man ought to offer God. Perhaps it is better to say it is a metaphor, for though it can descend to ludicrous parody, it can also rise to heights of unselfish service and poetic grandeur, so much so that it can deceive us into thinking it is the highest good life has to offer, and worthy of being made into a religion.

Because of its fascination and power, romantic love tempts us to believe that it is what we were made for, that it alone can be the true fulfillment of our craving to love and be loved. This power to deceive and tempt makes it a dangerous form of love, yet because it is an analogy for the love between God and the soul, it can also inspire, enlighten and inform.

The origins of romantic love seem difficult to locate, but certainly there is some connection with medieval ideas and customs.

In the early Middle Ages there grew up an elaborate, ritualistic relationship between the sexes called "courtly love." It seems that much of what later came to be called "romantic love" derived from this. An examination of the hallmarks of courtly love is opposite to our theme because it developed in a Christian society and strangely parodied many of the religious beliefs and practices of the time, entailing "a flagrant contradiction between doctrine and manners,"[1] and encouraging a pagan element in the worship of Amor, the god of Love.

The main characteristics of courty love were these: (a) There was a strong religious element centered round service of the god of Love (Amor, Cupid, Venus) in whom the lover must have faith. There were hymns to love, a liturgy, ritual and laws of amatory activities, and these often appeared blasphemous.

(b) The Lady, as mistress in the feudal castle, was an object of exalted worship. She was represented as perfect in all her virtues and expected and received abject humility from her lover, his devoted service even to death, his unquestioning obedience to all her desires, his unfailing constancy, his acceptance of rebuke, coldness and caprice from her as her right.

(c) Since the love was adulterous, secrecy was essential to preserve the Lady's honor, though she usually had one confidant. Her role was to appear unattainable, and then gradually to accept her lover into varying degrees of intimacy that yet always retained the positions of object to be worshipped and worshipper.

(d) It was taught that love could not be resisted. It was a dark fate and an all-powerful deity who must be obeyed. It was also a sickness, and the lover was expected to exhibit the conventional symptoms of pallor, loss of appetite, distractedness, sleeplessness, inarticulateness, trembling and sighing in the presence of his Lady, even madness and final wasting away into death as a martyr to love.

(e) At the same time love was ennobling, the source of courtesy, virtue, faithfulness (of lover to Lady, not of Lady to husband) and self-oblation. It was inherently tragic, an obsession regarded as a noble sorrow when the Lady proved uncompliant.

(f) It was sensual and passionate but at the same time idealized, tender, exalted, poetic, solemn, considerate and ritualistic — passion purified and ennobled — and therefore a blessed gift. Its fulfillment was the reward given by the Lady to a faithful and devout lover, and not dutifully as to a husband, but freely as her right to bestow or withhold.

It can be seen how many of the above traits have been incorporated into literature and art from medieval times to our own. The twentieth century has not been a romantic age since the time of the post 1914-1918 war disillusionment, yet the glorification of adultery and the cult of the right of passionate love to make its own laws in disregard of all demands and duties other than its own persist. We even have the bizzare cult of the hippie commune where pathological criminals like Charles Manson are worshipped and obeyed as Jesus figures, though they are obviously purveyors of Satanism. "Evil be thou my good," as Milton's Satan says.

In other words, the tendency of the human heart to worship still continues and is still misdirected to the human instead of to God.

St. Paul wrote to the Romans: "They exchanged the glory of the immortal God for a worthless imitation, for the image of mortal man . . . they have given up divine truth for a lie and have worshipped and served creatures instead of the Creator. . . . Since they refused to see it was rational to acknowledge God, God has left them to their own irrational ideas and to their monstrous behavior" (Rom. 1.23,25,28).

He is referring to literal idol worship, yet the words could well be applied to many of the cults of the twentieth century where human relationships of one kind or another become an end in themselves, and are adorned with many of the trappings of religion.

[111]

In a more subtle and often poetically disguised way, romantic love still coaxes the impulse to worship from its rightful end. Such love now bears little outward resemblance to the ritualistic customs of the twelfth century, yet many of the ideas have carried over in modernized forms.

It could be said that the person who passes through life without ever experiencing that state called "being in love" has missed out on a vital enrichment of personality. Yet it is noticeable that there are few cases of enduring conjugal love in which the "being in love" that first drew the couples together, persists. It seems that the everyday realistic situations of matrimony dispel the intoxication with the ideal, replacing it by something both more humdrum, enduring and reliable.

What is it that people experience when they fall romantically in love?

Temporarily at least they are often lifted from the plane of ordinary existence into a heightened awareness. They may discover in themselves poetic impulses and may even try to write poetry extolling the beloved's beauties and virtues, and expressing the tumult and power of their own emotions.

They become capable of an intensity of feeling and desire that they would not have thought possible. It is rather like being born anew in a newly-discovered world. They see beauty where before they were oblivious of it. They seem more alive than ever before, and all their senses more active. Their imaginations are stimulated so that they discover analogies for their love in the natural world, with a consequent strong sense of being one with the universe, a universe joyously conniving in this miracle of love.

They are ruled by one obsession — to be near the beloved, who seems a mine of treasures and fascinations yet to be uncovered. They believe they would never tire of being with her, that her least gesture and world are unique.

The desire to serve, to be subject to the beloved, even to abase oneself, is often present. The lover rises to heights of self-sacrifice he never thought possible. He loves to do for her sake whatever is repugnant or troublesome as a proof of love and to win her approval.

Both lovers may have a sense of predestination, mutually agreeing that they have been chosen for, and guided by God or Fate towards each other. Because of this they have a right to flout convention, to disregard other ties of duty or custom, in order to make their love of first importance in their lives and a means of mutual fulfillment. Love is honoring them by using them, and they are bound to follow where he leads. They feel at times like sacrificial victims (especially if their love is illicit), in their compulsion to obey the dictates of their love, no matter whose lives, including theirs, are ruined as a result. They are prepared to be made martyrs to love, and may often have a morbid preoccupation with suffering, believing that anguish is nobler than happiness, and a proof of the reality and intensity of love.

In fact, each is possessed by the other, and by their passion itself. Their actions are not the result of rational decision, but of blind impulse propelling them towards each other. They are the victims of an obsession, but they give it much grander names than that.

It follows that romantic love is possessive in the extreme. The idea of sharing the beloved with another is both abhorrent and painful. Jealousy is easily aroused and often in trivial pretexts. Its intensity may be such as to drive the lover to violent acts against the rival, the beloved, and/or himself. Reason has abdicated in favor of passion.

> My love is as a fever, longing still
> For that which longer nurseth the disease;
> Feeding on that which doth preserve the ill,
> The uncertain sickly appetite to please.
> My reason, the physician to my love,
> Angry that his prescriptions are not kept,
> Hath left me, and I desperate now approve.
> Desire is death, which physic did except.
> Past cure I am, now Reason is past care,
> And frantic-mad with evermore unrest;
> My thoughts and my discourse as madmen's are,
> As random from the truth vainly express'd;

> For I have sworn thee fair, and thought thee bright,
> Who art as black as hell, as dark as night.[2]

The swing in the final couplet from the one extreme of celebrating the beloved as the amalgam of all beauties and goodness, to the other of cursing her as evil and destructive, is typical of romantic love. It is divorced from realism and reason, and so always tends to see in stark black and white, rather than in varying degrees of grey.

By contrast, here is the gentle realism of the opening lines of W. H. Auden's "Lullaby":

> Lay your sleeping head, my love,
> Human on my faithless arm . . .

and his bald statement from "One Evening":

> O stand, stand at the window
>   As the tears scald and start;
> You shall love your crooked neighbor
>   With your crooked heart.

This poetic vision acknowledges the reality of original sin and the consequent defilement of the human heart (whatever terminology it uses), but romanticism denies this truth of the human condition. Instead it believes in the perfectibility of man without the aid of grace, and obsessively seeks to locate and adore this perfection in human beings, with the consequent fierce disillusionment expressed in Shakespeare's sonnet. This last can be the source of a romantic melancholy and cultivation of suffering for suffering's sake as a noble emblem of the lover's otherworldliness and fine sensitivity.

There is an element of fateful compulsion in romantic love. Even when the idol falls, it is still an idol, but with feet of clay. The bitter disillusionment and pain does not necessarily free the worshipper, or prevent him from seeking a substitute idol. The impulse to adore demands an outlet, and will have it in a human if denied it in God. "The Lord looks into men's hearts and finds there illusion" (Ps. 93).

It follows that romanticism encourages role-playing. Just as the medieval lover was expected to adhere to a certain pattern of behavior, so the modern romantic tends to play roles — The Tragedy Queen; The Master of Misery; The Hermit Crab; The Unappreciated Martyr; The Victim of the Fatal Passion; The Hypersensitive Heart; The Wooer of Unattainable Women; The Doormat Adorer. The variations are multitude, according to the temperament and character traits of both lover and beloved. In each case, role-playing fastens the lover to his own mechanisms. He has sacrificed his freedom, and until he learns to practice dissociation from his role, refusing to say "I" to it, he will know neither true peace nor true love.

To indulge the affection of love means to use another person as an outlet for one's affective emotions. For all its proud protestations of self-

[116]

sacrifice and devotion, romantic love is a system of animus-anima projections, where both lover and beloved seek to assuage deep, personal needs and to fulfill hidden hungers in themselves. Thus they treat love as a commodity to be used, and each other as a means to be manipulated to the end of their own self-satisfaction.

This innate selfishness is concealed under high-sounding, idealistic talk of sacrifice even to the point of dying for the beloved. The fact is not faced that it would be much easier to accept reality and live for an imperfect, basically flawed beloved in the abrasive, everyday intimacies of Christian marriage.

Romantic love's aversion to reality derives largely from its association with fantasy and dream. The lover projects onto the beloved from his own interior world and imagination, what he wants to find in her, and proceeds to love it. The aim is to glamorize the real and merely human, to inject the extraordinary into the ordinary. Consequently the beloved often becomes "la princesse lointaine" – an unattainable ideal of mystery and magic to be adored from afar.

La princesse lointaine for her part becomes the Sleeping Beauty dreaming of the Fairy Prince. All that would keep them apart – duty, convention, ethics, religious principles, other people – is seen as the cruel hedge of thorns that deserves to be demolished for the sake of love.

This intoxicated dreaming, or dreamy intoxication,

can become an unhealthy obsession of the imagination. It is true that out of it have sprung some of the world's greatest works of art − but it has also been the seed bed of much misery and evil. It can even lead to an exaltation of the state of madness, and to a deliberate effort to escape from reality into this dream world of trance and illusion via drugs.

Associated with it is excessive, narcissistic introspection, and a desire for solitude and silence because one can most readily retire into this interior realm of Keat's "perilous seas in faery lands forlorn" and remain immersed in fantasy when alone. The romantic lover is an egotist, wearing his bleeding heart upon his sleeve and completely preoccupied with his own feelings, sufferings, exaltations, visions and projections. Yet he will maintain that he alone is capable of noble self-sacrifice and uttermost giving. But then the world − meaning the ordinary clodhoppers, living outside his own charmed orbit − is incapable of understanding a heart as sensitive, inspired and extraordinary as his.

He is really in love with his own idea of love, and not with a human beloved at all, and unless he faces up to this basic dissociation from reality, he will never learn to love in the way Jesus told us to.

Irving Babbitt[3] says that romantic love is a confusion of the planes of being, "the terrestrial and the heavenly." He draws a parallel with medieval courtly love, explaining how "sense is pressed into the service of spirit at the risk of perilous confusion" so as "to give sense a sort of infinitude."

Romantic love is secular, and yet sets itself "above the law of measure." Imagination is deliberately used "to enhance emotional intoxication" and "to pursue an illusion for its own sake" in "the never-ending quest after the ever-fleeting object of desire."

It is "a dalliance of the imagination with its own dream . . . the cherishing of glamor."

It may seem that what has so far been written in this chapter has nothing to do with the theme of the purification of the heart and with the love of God, but this is a mistake.

The fact is that a person may be born with a romantic temperament and set out to pursue God rather than a human beloved as depicted above. This kind of temperament meets a different kind of obstacle and temptation in the spiritual life from a naturally colder, more analytical, less imaginative and less sensuous nature.

The romantic's natural longing for the ideal, the unattainable, the mysteriously compelling, the beauty that can never fade, predisposes him to hunger and seek for God if religion becomes a reality in his life. As noted, the romantic's way of falling in love with a human beloved is the closest human analogy to the mystic's way of falling in love with God. After all, it is the Song of Songs, that oriental, passionate, sensuous, romantic love poem, that is scripturally interpreted as depicting the ardent soul's searching for and fusion with the divine Beloved.

The idyllic, lyrical quality in romantic love lifts the lover out of the commonplace into the ethereal and magic, and such a temperament, not being slave to the rational and literal, readily accepts the mystery and transcendence of God, and is drawn by them to seek him.

However, just because it is naturally poetic and mystical, it is also easily misled into illusion. It tends to misread experiences in prayer and in human relationships, mistaking the sensible for the spiritual. It also tends to value the sensible too highly, because its innate emotionalism, responsiveness and sensuousness makes it react strongly and positively to such consolations. It easily becomes greedy, seeking and clinging to such experiences and relationships for their own sakes, instead of disregarding them as the accidents of the true union of the soul with God through a perfectly submissive will. It mistrusts a love that is dry and unemotional, yet it is precisely in this way that it has to learn to love in its purification.

Such a heart may romanticize our Lord, pretending he is always "gentle Jesus meek and mild," the friend of sinners, sweet and undemanding and in no way terrible and strong. It evades the horror of Christ's passion, which he invites us all to join, in favor of those incidents in our Lord's life — his blessing of children, his healing of the sick, his promises of comfort — that do not summon us to suffer and die with him.

This romanticism is carried over into personal relationships in a tendency to idealize. It believes it is seeing Christ in others when it does this, but again it is the fatal drive to make a Christ-idol out of a human being, and worship it. Much suffering and training in self-honesty has to be endured before such a temperament can see and love the beloved human in all his faults and weaknesses and without illusion, and at the same time acknowledge and revere the presence of the divine through grace in him.

Here I emphasize that it is not just love between the sexes that can be romanticized, but any human relationship at all, including devotion to causes. Wherever there is any attempt to glamorize, there is romanticism.

The romantic who is not religious is often a devotee of humanism and humanitarianism. He believes in the perfectibility of man if only social conditions were altered, or we went "back to nature." Similarly, the religious romantic can easily put the second commandment before the first, become emotionally involved in an idealistic fashion with those he loves and/or helps, and soon drift from God. He is then making a religion out of love by thinking the emotion of loving, the intoxication of giving, and the intensity of his craving, are what God wants of him. He does not realize that what he must do is go against this natural trend, disidentify with it, and by the help of grace become detached and calm so that his human relationships are not one huge distraction and excuse for not getting on with the real business of his heart's purification.

Most of the characteristics of the romantic lover listed here in this chapter can evince themselves in one disguise or other in both our relationships with God and with neighbor, if we have that kind of temperament and are not on guard against it. And yet the same qualities can be of immense help in exactly the same areas, when imbued with grace, modified and used in accordance with God's will and solely for his honor and glory.

The romantic heart's prayer must be: "Indeed you love truth in the heart, then in the secret of my heart teach me wisdom. O purify me, then I shall be clean (of all my illusions); O wash me, I shall be whiter than snow" (Ps. 50).

After all, it was St. John of the Cross who himself wrote, and used for his exposition of spiritual betrothal and marriage, an ardent love song.

My lov'd one is in the hills,
The lonely valleys clad with forest-trees,
The rushing, sounding rills,
Strange isles in distant seas,
Lover-like whisperings, murmurs of the breeze.

My love is hush-of-night,
Is dawn's first breathings in the heav'n above,

Still music veil'd from sight,
Calm that can echoes move,
The feast that brings new strength — the feast of love.

Now blooms our nuptial bed,
Safe-hid from men by lions' fortress-lair,
With royal purple spread,
Builded all free from care,
Crown'd with a thousand golden scutcheons rare. . . .

11

THE INORDINATE NEED FOR LOVE –
The Greedy, Insecure, Hungry Heart

IT is right, natural and necessary that human beings should want and need to love and be loved. It is when this need becomes inordinate and the motive for most of what we do and strive for, that the heart is being deflected from God.

What is meant here is an emotional craving that is excessive and at least largely involuntary. I hesitate to use the label "neurotic," for the point at which neurosis proper begins is hard to define. Also where grace is strongly at work, neuroses are often its chief targets, and in the process of becoming grace-imbued they change their nature and characteristics.

Added to this, we are all "queer" in some way or another. No human being is "normal" in the sense of being completely balanced, for all originate from and are nurtured by parents or parent-substitutes who are themselves deviations through the fall from God's norm for man – integrity, right order and interior harmony.

"The primordial sin, because it was the rejection of sanctifying grace, destroyed man's centeredness in

God, and is precisely disintegration. . . . Psychological disorder, in the broadest sense, is thus 'normal', and indeed universal for fallen man, that is to say, for empirical man as we know him. His nature is not destroyed: none of his essential parts is eliminated, but they *are* disorganized. . . . Still more do the living parts and faculties of human nature, deprived of their center and the power of grace which bound them equitably together, tend to fly off in different directions, and at each other's expense in innumerable different ways. While not all these may be, by psychiatric standards, pathological, some may very well be so. Original sin, as the absence of the original integrity, is not the cause of particular ailments; but particular ailments with their particular causes would not exist except for the disorganization, the sickness of nature, which is common to us all."[1]

When the need to love and be loved is inordinate, it is coupled with emotional insecurity, the feeling and conviction of being unloved and unwanted. Its origin is nearly always in unsatisfactory and unsatisfying nurture in early childhood.

What would be for other people an ample degree, intensity and proof of love, is never enough for the emotionally insecure heart. It is insatiable in its need because it can never really believe it is loved. For the same reason it makes impossible demands and, under all kinds of guises, persists in trying people out to see at what stage they will decide they have had enough and administer the reproof or rejection that this heart constantly fears will come.

This basic insecurity evinces itself in a bewildering variety of symptoms from greedy over-eating to obsessive phobias, from functional disorders to advanced escape mechanisms merging into the psychotic.

The heart may veer from one extreme of being incapable of giving generously and without bargaining, to the other of an inability to control giving so that it goes to excesses, and embarrasses or frightens the recipient of its love. It may be compelled to put up and keep intact barriers that prevent both the entrance of others into its depths and sensitivities, and its own emergence from itself to mingle freely with another in the intimate and fruitful exchanges of love.

It may irritate others with the persistence of its efforts to give itself, coupled with its intense possessiveness and jealousy. It may develop a "grand passion" based on illusion. Here, a projection is made upon another of the heart's own impossible ideal of a lover who fulfills every one of its exorbitant needs. It is this projection that arouses the devouring, intense passion, not the faulty human being who is clothed in it and made unrecognizable.

Whether it withdraws or throws itself at others, this heart is inordinate in both its affections and its expectations.

It also carries a crippling load of anxiety centered

on the fear of rejection. Sometimes it behaves in the way most likely to realize its fears, because once the worst actually happens, at least one is temporarily free of the dread that it may happen.

It also challenges the love object by capricious, irritating, selfish, demanding and taunting behavior, as if it were saying, "I'm being as bad as I can be — dare you to reject me!"

If not rejected, it may then indulge in tearful reconciliations, abject apologies and sincere promises never to "carry on like that again."

But because its behavior is mechanistic, it does of course do the same things all over again before very long, for it can never rest at peace in the certainty of being loved. Always it must test and challenge love, forcing it into a retaliatory or defensive position if possible.

Then it can say, "I knew you didn't really love me. It was all a sham. You didn't mean what you said. You only want to be rid of me!" — and so make for itself an excellent excuse for a suffocating bout of obsessive misery.

Once rebuff or rejection actually happens, and the heart's worst fears are realized, it may collapse into apathy and depression, even into despair with suicidal undertones. In its desolation it is convinced that no one in the whole world loves or wants it, that it is unworthy of love anyway, that it is unlovable, contemptible, a failure and an object of mockery.

Sometimes it dreads going out and being seen at all

for fear of the mockery its false imagination conjures up. Many a recluse becomes so as a result of some such pattern of behavior.

Other times, its need for love prevents it from being able to be alone, making it compulsively gregarious. It must continue its search for the ideal, perfect love that will meet all its insatiable demands, but ask nothing in return.

Oblivious that it manipulates and uses others, or aware but unable to control the tendency, it perhaps sets out to impress, to arouse admiration and interest, by dramatic role-playing or window-dressing. Whether this takes the form of self-aggrandizement or self-abasement, its aim is like that of the Venus insect-killer plant − to entice, to entrap, to suck dry, to eject when of no more use.

The inordinate need to be loved must be met, and on the insecure heart's own terms.

Because excessive importance is assigned to being liked, loved, appreciated, praised, fondled, protected, this heart evaluates itself in relation to how much of these reactions it can provoke in others. If it can find no one to love it and meet its demands, it is eaten up by a feeling of inferiority. It has failed to attain success in the only activity that can prove it worthy, and even self-hatred may be the result.

All this is bound up with the painful need for reassurance. This heart has no objective, detached evaluation of personal worth, it cannot love itself charitably and with good-humored acceptance. It is compelled either to overvalue or undervalue itself. Either way, it needs constant reassurance from someone else whom it respects and in whose love it believes — however briefly.

It almost feels it has no right to be at all unless another affirms its worth as an individual.

"The difference between love and the neurotic need for affection lies in the fact that in love the feeling of affection is primary, whereas in the case of the neurotic the primary feeling is the need for reassurance, and the illusion of loving is only second-ary."[2]

Bound up with this need for reassurance and love is resentment and hostility at having to abase itself, trade, act a part and put itself in the power of another to get what it wants. It will even be perverse enough to punish the very person who bestows the craved reassuring love, because anyone who could love one as despicable as itself must himself be despicable!

For such a heart there is neither peace nor rest. One is reminded of St. John of the Cross's vivid metaphor: "But the other man loses everything, running to and fro upon the chain by which his heart is attached and bound; and with all his diligence he can still hardly free himself for a short time from this bond of thought and rejoicing by which his heart is bound."[3]

Such a heart is enchained by its obsessive, inordinate desire to be loved and to be reassured that it is worthy of love. Yet it is usually quite blind to the fact that it cannot love anyone itself. It may both want and try to love, yet true love's selfless, disinterested acceptance and cherishing of another for his own sake and not because of what can be got out of him, is not within such a heart's capabilities.

"Many such relations are carried on under the camouflage of love, that is, under a subjective conviction of attachment, when actually the love is only the person's clinging to others to satisfy his own needs. That this is no reliable feeling of genuine affection is revealed in the ready revulsion that appears when any wishes are not fulfilled. One of the factors essential to our idea of love — reliability and steadiness of feeling — is absent in these cases."[4]

As is to be expected, because of its painful insecurity such a heart is hypersensitive. The least reproof is interpreted as wholesale rejection, a slight abstraction as final withdrawal of love, the mildest disagreement as the end of the relationship, a passing interest in another person as a casting-off of itself, a good-natured criticism as an unbearable insult, an offhanded remark as a deliberate, deadly humiliation.

It is obvious that false imagination plays a lively role in the inordinate need for love. It fosters irrationality, blurs distinctions between gradations, blows up the trivial to exaggerated importance and encourages endless dramas and role-playing.

A quite unreal world can be created, a world in which balance, proportion, truth and honesty play little part. And yet nowhere here are there deliberate lies.

Karen Horney nicely summarizes this heart's affliction as "an over-evaluation of the factual significance of being liked."[5] This does not sound serious, yet such a distortion of emphasis can lead to any or all the evils listed above, and many others not touched upon.

What can be done to remedy the situation?

Such emotional sickness may be severe enough to need psychotherapy. It may or may not benefit psychologically as a result.

However, this book is concerned with the cleansing of such a heart in a spiritual sense. Whether or not psychotherapy is resorted to, and is or is not helpful, the work of purifying the heart's relationship in charity to God and neighbor is in a different category.

At the outset, one thing must be made clear, since it is not a deliberately sinful heart that is under consideration here, but one that is afflicted and can do little or nothing (until it is shown how) to alter the pattern of its mechanisms. Victor White puts it succinctly.

"The fact that a neurotic, more or less unconsciously, is commonly found to have a certain 'need to be ill' on account of the advantages which his illness brings him, and the defenses with which his neurosis provides him, does not contradict the fact that the neurotic structure and its symptoms are unwilled by his conscious ego."[6]

Although I am avoiding the word "neurotic," the kind of behavior listed here is certainly not fully deliberate.

It is unlikely that the heart that enters the dark night would have anything like the intensity and variety of symptoms and mechanisms described here, though it is worth nothing that some experts agree that neuroses, and even psychoses, are not incompatible with sanctity.

"Moreover even if one does not go so far as to say with the psychoanalyst that we all have some pathological tendency, it must be admitted that these tendencies are widely distributed in our poor human nature, and that they now form part of the consequences of original sin, which singularly burden it. These tendences exist in various degrees — in a benign state most of the time, more or less hidden from ourselves, if not from others, under our daily routines, in the inner subjections or endurances that we impose upon ourselves, or better in the compensations that we seek or that we demand of our entourage. . . . The purification of the spirit brings to the surface with a painful awareness these tendencies deeply rooted in the faculties."[7]

In the pages that follow, Father Marie-Eugene goes on to state that it can be difficult to distinguish between the effects of the dark night and those of mental illness. Yet, "when one has assurance that the soul is advancing towards God, it is high wisdom not to linger over the least psychological troubles that may appear, probing into their origin and nature. This is so, given the fact that as a general rule they bear some resemblance with certain disorders of psychosis and are rather frequently intermingled with them to some degree, and given especially that the most efficacious means of curing them is in the orientation of the soul to God alone, 'the perfect health of the soul' ".[8]

He explains how the patient bearing of the humiliations and sufferings arising out of such disturbances is a valuable means of growth in virtue and holiness. He refers to "real holiness which is measured by charity and can be found together with pathological effects, and not of canonized holiness which, in order to be proposed for the veneration and imitation of the faithful, must normally be free of all that could tarnish it or diminish it in the judgment of men."[9]

It is unlikely that anyone but a gifted director would be able to discern genuine holiness in a disturbed personality manifesting itself in bizarre or unbalanced ways. Yet this does not deny its presence. As long as the disturbances of behavior are involuntary, and the sufferer never deliberately wills them, grace can be bringing the unafflicted side of his nature to high perfection.

"And even though such a disorder may bring about

[133]

involuntary disordered attitudes and behavior, we have no right on their account to suppose that the sanctifying processes of grace are absent, even though the disorders may prevent their outward manifestation. It may well be that it is in and through those disorders that the life of grace is operative, and that the very disorders contribute to the sanctification, whether they be due to a virus, to bacilli, or to a father-fixation."[10]

The heart that is afflicted by the inordinate need for love with all the imbalances arising from it, is not cut off from grace because of its emotional disturbances. Instead, if it truly wants, wills and tries to love God and neighbor, it cannot help but receive an abundance of grace and a consequent cleansing, even though some of the symptoms distressingly persist.

It can be paralleled with bodily cancer. The sufferer receives all the grace he pleads for to help him bear his pain patiently, humbly and bravely, but it is most unlikely that the cancer itself will be divinely healed.

As well, it must be obvious that an affliction like the inordinate need for love described here, is just as likely to be worked on by grace and become a means of sanctification as a physical illness or bodily affliction.

The first thing that has to be done, as in the Alcoholics Anonymous program, is to admit that one's heart is to a greater or lesser degree controlled by mechanisms to which it must submit instead of having freedom of choice.

Then, having acknowledged helplessness, the heart must do two things — work in some way, however small, to replace the mechanistic reactions and actions by consciously willed ones, and plead for and rely on grace both to do this and to suffer humbly all that cannot be changed.

It must pray to the Spirit for light upon its condition and upon what to do about it, at the same time detachedly observing (not analyzing) the mechanistic pattern. With regard to this, detachment can be developed merely by saying, "What is *it* doing?" rather than, "What am *I* doing?"

Sometimes enlightenment will be given so that the complete behavior pattern is seen, with all its ramifications. Such a bird's-eye view is invaluable as a guide to what has to be worked against and prayed for. It may be that the whole mechanism can be grouped round the same four passions that St. John of the Cross teaches we must learn to control by will.

A typical rejection mechanism might then be seen to work as follows:

Psychological imbalance: severe emotional insecurity arising from early childhood traumas.
This provokes *compulsive and obsessive need* to seek emotional security. *The means* sought is a reciprocal human love in which all insatiable demands are met.

Associated cravings: to feel permanently secure and safe in union with another in love; to be valued and convinced of worthiness because loved; to have this love victoriously survive all tests and trials; to have the sense of failure and defeat expunged by being loved; to escape from all that wounds and humiliates by being enfolded and clasped in love.

Attachment is felt for the one who is satisfying this obsessive need, to such a degree that to lose him would be a major disaster and might even provoke a breakdown or despair.

Self-seeking to get emotional security through this other, to manipulate, use and ensnare him so as to keep him as the source of reassurance, to have one's own love valued and cherished as proof that one is capable of love and not merely selfishly and immaturely possessive. Involved are *the four passions:*

> *Fear* of rejection, loss of security and the humiliation of rebuff or criticism;
>
> *Hope* that this love will prove to be all that is desired, that it will last till death, that it will never reveal any flaws, that it will be perfectly satisfying in every way;
>
> *Joy* when the need for reassurance and reciprocity is met, and when it seems one's hopes are being fulfilled and one's fears proved groundless;
>
> *Grief* to an intolerable degree if rejection (imagined or real) occurs, if the love is revealed as merely human and fallible, if the lover is unfaithful or loses interest, if one's own uncontrollable mechanisms are seen to be wrecking the relationship.

[136]

Illusion because the aroused passions and emotions, and the inordinate love needs cloud reason, provoke false imagination, get values wrong, push everything out of proportion, and idealize the lover.
Loss of peace and detachment as a result of all the above.

Even if only one habitual reaction can be isolated (for example, that of becoming depressed and humiliated if criticized in any way) and worked upon, the mechanism is cracked and may well eventually crumble away.

It will be observed that feelings of depression and humiliation express themselves in an interior monologue that goes on monotonously and involuntarily, usually making up accounts, assigning praise and blame, composing recriminations and reproaches, wailing self-hatred and self-accusations, intoning dirges about one's worthlessness and the pointlessness of living.

The method is to observe these repetitive songs and recitations and deliberately replace them by positive thoughts: "I am a child of God, and God loves me; I am safe in the arms of Jesus; Mary holds me to her mother's heart; no one can harm me because God is protecting me always, whatever happens."

Or else one replaces them by direct prayer: "Lord, accept my suffering as part of your own agony at rejection, and your own humiliation; I offer it to you in reparation for my own and others' sins; dear Lord, stay close to me because I'm helpless without you; Jesus, I'm afraid of depression and despair, but I trust in you to lead me through the darkness into your light and love; Jesus, no one loves me, no one can put up with me, and the misery of rejection is more than I can bear — but I know and affirm that you love me, that you'll never betray or reject me. Please make your love an actuality to me, and help me trust heroically in you."

This deliberate turning of emotional suffering into positive affirmation and prayer is an exercise in faith, hope and charity. It cannot help but purify this heart of at least some of its inordinate need.

When "the first movement of the heart towards creatures" is detected, that is, the first involuntary attraction towards a new love object who it is hoped will appease the heart's longings for comfort, reassurance and security, a deliberate and immediate turning to our Lord must be practiced.

"Lord, here I go again, off to build another idol and place my peace at the disposal of another fallible human being. I don't want to be distracted from you like this. I don't want to be the victim of this mechanism. I know and affirm that only you can meet my heart's insatiable demands. So please give me the grace to resist this attraction; to refuse to give this person power over me; to acknowledge before I begin that disillusionment and anguish will be the inevitable results from the entanglement I'm in such danger of seeking; and to have the strength to say no to this urge in me to seek security where it can't be found. Alone, I am completely weak and helpless, Jesus. You must make your strength perfect in my weakness, or I'll go on betraying you and myself all over again. Help me, Lord."

If such prayer is persisted in, and the sacraments are sought, and relied upon, the time will probably come when, just as the alcoholic or drug addict refuses the drink or the fix, so this heart refuses its own form of addiction — emotional entanglement and dependence upon another human being for security, peace and well-being.

This is to replace the automatic, mechanical, habitual reaction and urge by a willed choice of God and detachment.

Since only God can fulfill our deepest needs, and the insecure heart's need is deeper than that of most others, it is a powerful form of re-education for this heart to act as if he actually were doing so, even though the emotions feel nothing but abandonment, desolation, loss and loneliness.

Ask, "If God were truly fulfilling my inordinate need for love and reassurance, how would I feel and act?"

And reply to oneself, "Of course I'd be happy. I'd rejoice in my certainty of his fatherly care. I'd thank and praise him for looking after and cherishing me.

I'd turn to him constantly in all my needs and sufferings, quite certain that he will never let me down or fail to meet my demands. I'd rest in him, at peace in his endless enfoldment of me. All right then, I'll do just that now, at this moment, and in the next moment as it comes, and the next. . . ."

If one has not a virtue, it is a good idea to act as one would if one did have it. The insecure heart lacks the virtue of trust. Deliberately to act as if it possessed this virtue, even while the emotions are clamoring their fears and apprehensions, is to possess what it feels it lacks.

The cultivation of the way of spiritual childhood, together with all that St. Thérèse has to teach about it, is immense help to such a heart. It capitalizes on its own inordinate needs by turning in its helplessness and weakness to the heavenly Father, and to Christ its Lord dwelling within it.

"I can do all things in Christ who strengthens me." The weak and helpless know they cannot endure for a moment, or do God's will at all without his help. They consciously draw and rely upon grace. They lay claim fiercely to God's promises of aid and our Lord's sublime affirmation, "Behold, I am with you all days, even to the end of the world."

They do not attempt to do great things for God, knowing their incapacity. Instead they labor at the minute conquests in keeping with their own smallness and powerlessness, offering tiny mortifications of self-pity, and penances of accepting their self-manufactured emotional sufferings, as the only gifts their inadequacy can produce.

They lean consciously on God second by second, the humiliation of their helplessness slowly turning into the peace of true humility.

"Craving for possession is one of the fundamental defenses against anxiety",[11] and therefore the insecure heart finds detachment from desires very difficult to cultivate. Non-possessiveness in the heart and will is for it an heroic attainment. Its cravings for the fulfilment of its emotional needs are inordinate, yet since they are involuntary they are not true moral ills.

The suffering that they cause can be a most valuable form of prayer, if it is accepted without self-pity and recrimination, and in union with Christ's redemptive sufferings. Some small self-conquest in this area that would seem entirely trivial to the psychologically robust, is for this heart a major attainment.

Complexes, compulsions, obsessions, can be worked upon by grace in the passive purgations until their very roots are dissolved away — if that is God's will. The insecure heart has to contribute to this work of grace by laboring to replace its constant cry of, "I want," into the willed desire, "I want you, God, and nothing and no one else."

Success is irrelevant really, and cannot be subjectively assessed anyway. It is the persistent effort, in spite of failures and apparent lack of progress, that matters. It is this effort, plus the direct hidden work of grace upon the heart, that leads to its purification, even though psychological imbalances may remain.

"For there is no going forth from the pains and afflictions of the secret places of the desires until these be mortified and put to sleep."[12] This is true, but it may be God's will for the emotionally wounded heart to go on bearing its "pains and afflictions" as the very means of its sanctification. The humiliation its spiritual and character imperfections and its personality disorders bring it, may lead it into such a depth of humility that it has no deliberate self-love or self-will left.

Such a heart has then been purified in its substance, though the accidents still evince a psychological illness.

EMOTIONAL INVOLVEMENTS
AND ATTACHMENTS

"INVOLVE-
MENT" is one of today's catch words. We are told we
must prove the reality of our religious commitment
through Christian involvement with people and their
problems. We are to exhibit a genuine concern and
make efforts to relate to others in order to prove our
interest and win their confidence. We are called upon
to renew the temporal order by the holiness of our
own lives and loves involving it.

All this is excellent, as long as the first commandment is never separated from the second.

Just as it is equally dangerous to love or not to
love, so it is just as hazardous to be involved as not to
be involved. If we carefully avoid involvement in
order to cultivate detachment, we run a serious risk
of affective dehydration and sinking into the selfish
mediocrity of playing safe. If we deliberately seek
involvement in order to express charity and prove
concern, we are likely to have our emotions aroused
and to find ourselves struggling hard against attachments that threaten peace of mind and heart.

How can we regulate our emotional involvements?

How can we learn to care and at the same time not to care?

Emotional involvements occur in all kinds of human relationships, and are usually the lubricant that keeps them going. If the members of a family were not emotionally involved among themselves there would be little dynamism in the family unit. The emotional involvement of lovers and friends is what knits them together. A man emotionally involved with the cause and the people he is fighting for, will last longer and suffer more for right and justice.

The person who is never emotionally involved with anyone or anything seems curiously dead and unattractive.

All these involvements and their variations are usually, like most human derivatives, a mixture of good and bad, of selfishness and altruism. It is when we seriously consider the nature of our loving, catch a glimpse of its impurities, and want to be cleansed of them, that we realize what a prison certain kinds of emotional involvements can make for us.

For convenience we can start with the traditional four passions of joy, hope, fear and grief, all of which are intense emotions, and see to what degree and in what manner they are present in involvements with causes and people.

These emotions (and the others in the range possible to us) can be either powerful allies or equally powerful hindrances to the will. For example, if the father of a family chooses a certain career and sets out to do well in it, his motives are usually a mixture of ambition, self-regard, and genuine desire to do the best he can for his wife and children. If this work gives him joy and satisfaction, if he is happy in it and has reason to hope for the kind of advancement that will not only be financial but open up even more opportunities for satisfaction, fulfilment and happiness, then these positive emotions are a real help towards application and effort.

If, on the other hand, he is caught up in some kind of work that is repugnant to him and in no way a source of emotional satisfaction, and he dare not leave it for fear of financial loss and harm to his family, then his negative emotional response does nothing to help give his will support in what he believes he must do. He fears to leave or lose his job, and all kinds of anxieties branch out as a result. His work makes him unhappy, and may even cause him grief, and from this arise resentment, bitterness and self-pity. He has nothing to hope from it except his pay packet and may well sink into a dull, routine inertia that is an undramatic form of despair.

In both situations there is emotional involvement and there are also dangers of a psychological and spiritual kind. Neither man is detached from his work. Although duty is involved in both cases, neither is at peace in his work because he sees it as God's will for him. One is seeking and gaining fulfilment, the other is deprived of it, but neither is related to God through what he is doing.

If, on the other hand, both were to see their work situation as their route to God, and one of their main ways of practicing self-abandonment to divine providence, there would be a shift of emphasis and a change in the nature of their emotional involvement.

If both had entered marriage as a Christian vocation and commitment, then the business of providing for wife and family would be an inseparable part of that vocation. It is good if we can do the kind of work that satisfies and fulfils our personalities and innate capacities. This is something to thank and praise God for. Our joy and hope in our work is then directed toward him as a prayer of thanksgiving. We see ourselves as stewards of whatever gifts God has built into our natures, and the careful development and application of these gifts is a way of glorifying and honoring him, not of building up our own self-esteem and helping us up the ladder of ambition.

And so our emotional involvement with our loved work does not stop short at the work itself but passes straight through it to God.

Paradoxically, it is equally good if circumstances force us into a kind of work that is antipathetic to us and gives us no joy or fulfilment. If intelligent efforts to find something more suitable fail, then we can, by accepting our unfortunate situation as God's training ground in virtue for us, turn it all to spiritual good.

The spontaneous negative emotional responses it arouses in us can be the means of secret immolation, penance and mortification of desire. We are given the opportunity for invaluable purification of the will by making acts of abandonment to divine providence when all our feelings are urging us to rebellion and bitterness. Our suffering and grief can be spiritualized and used redemptively by seeing them as part of the Savior's suffering and grief, of his passion — that work so repugnant to his natural emotions, and so fertile for the salvation of the world.

This attitude is not one of spineless resignation. There is no reason why such a man should not keep alert to any possibilities of escape from the hated situation, but at the same time his acceptance of it, for as long as it must continue, as God's way of training his heart and will and making them supple, stops negative emotions from turning sour within him.

It is the spiritualization of the work situation, whether it is a pleasant or an unpleasant one, which will help to bring about that renewal of the secular order that Vatican II stressed was the layman's proper sphere.

"It is ordinarily by his labor that a man supports himself and his family, is joined to his fellow men and serves them, and is enabled to exercise genuine charity and be a partner in the work of bringing God's creation to perfection. Indeed, we hold that by

[147]

offering his labor to God a man becomes associated with the redemptive work itself of Jesus Christ. . . .

In the exercise of all their human activities, they can thereby gather their humane, domestic, professional, social, and technical enterprises into one vital synthesis with religious values, under whose supreme direction all things are harmonized to God's glory. . . .

After acquiring whatever skills and experience are absolutely necessary, they should in faithfulness to Christ and his gospel observe the right order of values in their earthly activities. Thus their whole lives, both individual and social, will be permeated with the spirit of the beatitudes, notably with the spirit of poverty. Whoever in obedience to Christ seeks first the kingdom of God will as a consequence receive a stronger and purer love for helping all his brothers and for perfecting the work of justice under the inspiration of charity."[1]

It begins to be obvious that the already stressed criterion applies here too: emotional involvement is good and spiritually healthy if it is directed towards the honor and glory of God, not towards self-aggrandizement.

"The strength of the soul consists in its faculties, passions and desires, all of which are governed by the will. Now when these faculties, passions and desires are directed by the will toward God, and turned away from all that is not God, then the strength of the soul is kept for God, and thus the soul is able to love God with all its strength."[2]

In gospel terms: "Seek first the kingdom of heaven, and the rest shall be added."

The four passions are aroused by all kinds of human successes and failures. They are part of our equipment for dealing with life. The point is – do we become immersed in them for their own sake and within the confinements of the human situation, or do we seek to purify them by lifting them up and relating them to God and the kingdom of heaven within? This is the difference between the right and the wrong kinds of emotional involvement.

Besides the work situation, the other commonest source of emotional involvement is the relation between the sexes in courtship and conjugal love.

Strange as it may seem, the exceedingly common human activity of falling in love it not a Christian one. On the contrary, it is part of the tendency of the fallen human heart to set up and worship idols, to become enslaved to desire and the affection of love.

It is a combination of glandular activity, animus-anima projection and fascination with a dream. It seldom stands up to the mundane and unavoidable associations of marriage, and though it may lead a few to glorify and honor God for the beloved, it captivates most in the wrong kind of emotional involvement.

It remains the usual door into marriage in our

Western culture, but if it does not soon change into something much more stable and realistic it is more likely to lead to divorce than to faithful, lifelong union.

Nevertheless, it is paradoxically true that the experience of being in love is the nearest human analogy to the spiritual experience of the soul's seeking and attaining union with God. Its poetry, mystery, transports and self-immolation indicate what the human heart is capable of if only it would direct its whole capacity for love towards its Creator instead of one of his creatures.

Courtship and marriage for Christians is meant to be a clearly recognized vocation, joyfully accepted as a direct route to God. Though many of the sensations of falling in love may be present, they do not stop at the human level but are recognized as part of the love call of the human heart to God, and of God's to it.

The lovers see their relationship and their emotional involvement with each other as their means of doing God's will and fulfilling his creative purpose for them. They believe the consummation of their love in marriage and family life will directly help them grow in love of God. They see it as the means of sanctifying themselves and each other, and of being a leaven in the social community.

They understand that Christian marriage is not meant to be contracted under the compulsive spell of mutual fascination and the craving to possess. It should be based not upon passion, but upon the desire to do God's will and upon recognition of a vocation. This spiritualizes their emotional involvement and certainly does not exclude great joy in sexual union, and in all the physical expressions of love and tenderness. It adds to these reverence and the sense of the sacred, so that they can truly be entered into to the honor and glory of God.

In such a marriage, the passions (strong emotions) of joy, hope, fear and grief, that bring so many to the marriage guidance counselor and the divorce court, become helps not hindrances. Their joy in each other is not a selfish, self-centered passion that can be a means of emotional blackmail, but a way of thanking and praising God for his gift of love. It does not make them feed upon the emotional satisfaction they derive from each other, till they are dependent upon it and feel life is not worth living if it ceases. On the contrary, it is diffused into a calm glow of happiness and peace in each other that imbues the marriage with the certainty of permanence.

Their hopes are centered not upon worldly successes that will give their marriage social status, upon having children who are a credit to them, upon retaining their physical attractiveness and sexual appeal so as their partner will not stray to someone else for satisfaction — but upon serving each other more and more selflessly, giving themselves more and more fully to each other, to their children and to their marriage. They do this not merely for their own happiness and fulfilment, but fundamentally because they recognize the beauty of such giving, and that it is a most powerful prayer of thanksgiving to God who gave them to each other in the first place.

They have no need to experience fear and grief over unfaithfulness, cruelty and casual indifference, for they do not inflict these curses upon each other. They believe that the essence of marriage is in the will to love each other till death. This love, they know, will often not be a satisfying emotion, but a deliberate practicing of virtue in the face of feelings of weariness, self-pity, anxiety and irritation. They acknowledge that they are both human and imperfect, but they believe in the abundance of God's grace and its power to help them make of their marriage a way to the kingdom of heaven within.

Such marriages may pass through all kinds of vicissitudes and experiences their own dark nights. Grief may come through illnesses, financial setbacks, afflicted children, or calamities of one kind or another. Yet they never break. Because they are true vocations faithfully lived, they always end by bringing the partners closer to God.

Here, one may note that the natural tendency for physical desire and sexual activity to lessen markedly in middle age, may be God's way of calling such couples to a completely celibate love that is even more fully their route to union with him.

They may then attain that state of interior right order where "the soul rejoices only in that which is purely the honor and glory of God, and hopes for naught else, neither grieves save for things that concern this, neither fears aught save God alone."[3] In other words, their hearts' four passions will have been purified. Their struggles in the training ground of their marriage have brought them to the state where they know and live the truth that "the whole business of attaining to union with God consists in purging the will from its affections and desires; so that thus it may no longer be a base, human will, but may become a divine will, being made one with the will of God."[4]

Whatever the type of emotional involvement in our wide range of possible human relationships, of which only one or two have been sketched here, the principle remains the same. We must never permit our emotional involvement to become so intense that it preoccupies us, distracts us from God, and even incites us to sin. If we are aiming at the kingdom of heaven within and love union with God, the emotions have to be disciplined, desires have to be mortified, attachments have to be kept under control.

REFERENCES

(*Note:* All quotations from St. John of the Cross are from the three volume Burns Oates & Washbourne edition, London, 1953. The following abbreviations are used: *Ascent* for *Ascent of Mount Carmel; D.N.* for *Dark Night of the Soul; Flame* for *Living Flame of Love; S.S.* for *Spiritual Sentences and Maxims; Canticle* for *Spiritual Canticle.*)

Chapter 1.

1.   Pope, *Essay on Man II,* L. 3-18.
2.   Vatican II, *The Church, 8.*
3.   *Ibid. The Church Today, 10, 11.*

Chapter 3.

1.   *S.S.,* 3, P. 234.
2.   *Ascent,* P. 18.
3.   *Ascent,* P. 23.

Chapter 4.

1.   *Ascent,* P. 29.
2.   Wordsworth, *Sonnet to Milton.*

Chapter 5.

1.   *Ascent,* P. 243.

Chapter 6.

1.   J.P. de Caussade, S.J., *Self-abandonment to Divine Providence,* Burns & Oates, London, 1959.

2. Quoted by von Balthasar, *Thérèse of Lisieux*, Sheed & Ward, London, 1953, P. 175, 178.
3. Op. Cit. P. 176, 180.
4. Op. Cit. P. 189.

Chapter 7.

1. *S.S.*, P. 225.
2. *Ascent*, P. 33.
3. *Ascent*, P. 42.
4. *Ibid*, P. 49.
5. *Ibid*, P. 44-45.
6. *Ibid*, P. 51.
7. *Ibid*, P. 52.

Chapter 8.

1. *Ascent*, P. 50.
2. St. Teresa of Avila, *Life*, Sheed & Ward, London, 1944, P. 155.
3. *Ibid.*
4. *Canticle*, P. 165.
5. *Ascent*, P. 249.
6. *Ibid.*
7. *Ibid*, P. 251.
8. *S.C.*, B, P. 345.
9. E.W. Trueman Dicken, *The Crucible of Love*, Darton, Longman & Todd, 1963, P. 340.
10. Shakespeare, *King Lear*, Act II, Sc. iv.
11. *Ibid*, Act IV, Sc. vii.

Chapter 10.

1. de Rougement, *Passion and Society*, Faber, London, 1962, P. 72.

2. Shakespeare, Sonnet CXLVII.
3. Irving Babbitt, *Rousseau and Romanticism*, Houghton Mifflin, (1919) 1957.

Chapter 11.

1. Victor White, O.P., *Soul and Psyche*, Collins & Harvill, London, 1960, Pp. 184-185.
2. Karen Horney, M.D., *The Neurotic Personality of our Time*, Kegan, Paul, Trench & Trubner, London, 1947, P. 131.
3. *Ascent*, P. 256.
4. Horney, op. cit., P. 110.
5. *Ibid*, P. 116.
6. White, op. cit. P. 298, note to Chapter 10.
7. P. Marie-Eugène, *O.C.D., I Am a Daughter of the Church*, Mercier, Cork, 1955, Pp. 355-356.
8. *Ibid*, Pp. 359-360.
9. *Ibid*, footnote, P. 367.
10. White, op. cit., P. 188.
11. Horney, op. cit., P. 127.
12. *Ascent*, P. 18.

Chapter 12.

1. *Church Today, 67, 43, 72.*
2. *Ascent*, P. 243.
3. *Ibid.*
4. *Ibid.*